We Believe

We Believe

An Elementary Re-Affirmation of the Fundamentals of the Evangelical Christian Religion

by

Theodore Huggenvik

Published by

AUGSBURG PUBLISHING HOUSE • MINNEAPOLIS, MINNESOTA

Printed and Manufactured in the United States of America by
Augsburg Publishing House, Minneapolis 15, Minnesota

Introduction

We Believe was written by Dr. Huggenvik to meet a definite and known need. Two recent developments in the church have called it forth.

The Lutheran Church is receiving into its membership today a great many people who have had very little opportunity to study the fundamental teachings of the Christian church previous to their interest in Lutheranism. Many of them come from among the unchurched millions in our land, but a very considerable number come from other denominations. True to its tradition which has always rightfully emphasized the command of the Lord "to teach them" the Lutheran Church has sought to prepare carefully such applicants for membership through a thorough course of instruction. This practice has been most fruitful. It has brought to literally thousands (about 7000 are so instructed each year in the Evangelical Lutheran Church) an understanding of the way of salvation so that church membership has become a deep, sincere, fellowship with God through personal faith in Jesus Christ as Savior and Lord. One of the most significant developments in the American church is this mounting, rapidly growing interest in such instruction. But the materials available for such have been limited in quantity and in scope.

There is also an increasing demand for study materials suitable for adult groups in the congregation. Many desire to restudy the fundamental teachings of the church.

Pastors report in many places large groups requesting materials that will state in a concise, clear, yet fairly extensive way, the principles upon which the church stands.

It was in recognition of these developments and to meet these apparent needs that the Commission on Evangelism and the Board of Parish Education requested Dr. Huggenvik to produce the study manual *We Believe*. His long teaching experience and his unusual ability to make contact with young

v

and old alike have combined to produce a book which we expect will be widely used to broaden and deepen the spiritual understanding of both new converts and long time members of the church. It is our conviction that Dr. Huggenvik has rendered the church a valuable service in producing *We Believe.*

E. C. REINERTSON

Preface

Parts of this handbook on the fundamentals of the Christian faith, as interpreted by Lutherans, were published as a series of articles in *The Lutheran Teacher* from October, 1948, to and including October, 1949. The articles have been revised and enlarged. Two of them have been kept in their original form. Some new chapters have been added.

It is hoped that this handbook might serve as a book of general information for church members who wish to review the content of the teachings of the church. Then it is particularly designed for those who would like to become members of our Evangelical Lutheran congregations, and who should know, *before* they become members, the fundamental beliefs of the church that they are about to join. The handbook might certainly also be used as a guide in classes in Christian doctrine where time would allow a great deal of supplementary reading and accompanying lectures by the instructor. The pastor who uses this handbook may combine certain chapters, divide others into two or three lessons, or assign some for home reading. Also in the case of a pastor who uses these chapters for an adult instruction manual, he will realize that they serve primarily as a possible guide in the arrangement of the material to be covered.

This manual deals with Biblical truth. And it is essentially an affirmation of such truth. The author himself, rather than the sponsors, must be held accountable for anything that might seem to be personal interpretations.

St. Olaf College
Northfield, Minnesota
Autumn, 1949

THEODORE HUGGENVIK

Table of Contents

PART THREE—LUTHER'S SMALL CATECHISM

PART ONE

Fundamental Doctrines

We Believe in God

I am the Lord thy God (Exodus 20:2).
*For he that cometh to God must believe
that he is, and that he is the rewarder of them
that diligently seek him* (Heb. 11:6).

WHY DO WE BELIEVE IN GOD?

It is as natural to say to God: Thou art! as to say to myself:
I am. The idea of God is the most fundamental in human existence. Non-Christians, even those who have no Bible, believe in God or gods. And in the case where the idea of God
gets mixed up with many gods, there is a feeling that back
of it all there is one supreme deity, one creator-God. (See
Acts 14 and 17.)

Man, universally, then, believes in the presence of a supreme power or powers which can influence his destiny. If he
then begins to ask himself why he should believe in a supreme
being the answers from the Christian point of view would include the following:

We believe in God because we cannot understand how the
universe could originate by itself (Rom. 1:20). It must have
had a beginning. It is therefore natural to believe in God as
creator.

We believe in God because there seems to be present everywhere the evidence of design, plan. Then there must be a
supreme personality who designed everything (Ps. 19; Ps. 24;
Ps. 91). Wherever there is a designer we know there is mind
and intellect and personality. A watch does not make itself.
It is carefully planned and made according to that plan.

We believe in God because we have a conscience (Rom. 2: 14-15). We know the difference between right and wrong. If there is no final judge to whom we are accountable why should we be judged by our conscience?

We believe in God because we believe in goodness, truth and beauty.

We believe in God because of the testimony of Jesus Christ who claimed and demonstrated that God was manifested in Him and by Him. Jesus said that He came from God, that He was God. In Jesus Christ God visited this world. Our God is God-in-Christ (John 1:18).

We believe in God because He is revealed in the Bible. (We shall see later why we believe the Bible to be God's self-revelation.)

We believe in God because God gives meaning to life. Most of the things we do are done because we believe that life has a meaning. But life can have no meaning unless there is an ultimate reality, unless there is a final goal. Life must be moving towards an ultimate reality

The Christian religion affirms that life has a meaning. That affirmation is based upon the Christian belief in a Triune God as revealed in the Holy Scriptures. If there is no God who "keeps watch above His own," life becomes what Ivar Aasen called it: "a meaningless mess, an endless turmoil."

The Christian believes in a God who has made the world, but who Himself is other than the world. The Christian does not believe in a God who can be identified with any one nation as Hitler taught. It was Rosenberg who suggested that if the German race should die, then God would die with it. No. The Christian believes in a God who transcends the world even while He is governing the world and is vitally interested in it.

Today it needs to be affirmed with power that God is not a product of man's interpretation of the behavior of the universe, but that He is a reality, independent of man and the world. It is true as a certain poet said:

> God is God were all men dead
> God is God were all countries void.

Such affirmation must be made over against the modern teaching of immanationism which identifies God with the universe, and makes the universe divine. That is the central teaching of the new paganism that has held sway in recent years. Pantheism and Christianity cannot agree. An impersonal God cannot call me to rise and follow Him. An impersonal God cannot create faith in my heart. And without faith it is impossible to please God.

We believe in God because we can experience His nearness, His care, His love. Millions of Christians, down the ages, have affirmed their experience of God. I *know* that my Redeemer liveth! I am assured, fully assured, that there is a God.

IN WHAT KIND OF GOD DO WE BELIEVE?

The Christian believes in a Triune God. That teaching is absolutely essential in a religion that is redemptive, a religion that offers salvation from sin. Fatherhood is understood through sonship. God the Father is creator. We need a creator-God, a Father-God. The world is not eternal. It had a beginning. That calls for a creator. But the creator-God of the Bible is a God who cares, a loving Father, but also a just God. This God has revealed His will to us in·a holy law. That law we have not kept. So we look for a remedy for sin. Christianity brings before us the redemption that is in Christ. But we become dull and careless in our faith. We need a power to rekindle the flame of faith. That power is found in the person of the Holy Spirit. He convicts of sin and leads us to Christ. He shows us through the Word what the Christian life is like and gives us power to live it.

So Christians believe in a Triune God: the Father who creates, the Son who redeems, the Holy Spirit who sanctifies. But since all of God is Triune there is full cooperation on the part of the persons of the Trinity in the things that are accomplished.

The teaching that God is Triune makes the humanizing of God impossible, as a certain mystic puts it.

Christians believe in a God who is utterly available. Though He is a transcendant God, He is near to all those who call upon Him.

Christians believe in a God who has spoken, who has revealed Himself. That revelation reached the climax in Jesus Christ, God's last word to this world. The complete record of God's self-revelation we have in the Holy Bible.

It is a glorious and meaningful thing to believe in God, Creator and Father, Redeemer and Sanctifier. Without faith in God, life can have no ultimate meaning; for from God we came and to Him we return.

As Christians we need to stress, in these times, the personality of God and His Tri-unity. Also we need to remember that God is love; but that does not detract in the least from the fact that God is a just God. Thus we need to instill in the minds of those whom we teach, both the fear (respect) of God and the love of God. The First Commandment is absolutely fundamental: fear, love, trust in God above all things.

So we meet a God who is above all—not the subject of the whims of man's imagination. He is an eternal reality apart from man. When we hear His holy law we understand something of His character and personality. In the Ten Commandments He reveals His will. For the God who is holy also wants men to be holy. In the Gospel God makes known His lovingkindness, His willingness to help those who fail.

WHAT DIFFERENCE DOES IT MAKE WHETHER I BELIEVE IN GOD OR NOT?

Everyone has a god of some kind in his life, something that he worships directly or indirectly, something or someone to which he yields supreme allegiance. And man does not rise any higher than the thing he worships. The God-concept one has determines one's character, one's outlook upon life.

Back of man's struggle for freedom stands God and man's faith in Him. We need to be responsible to One higher than ourselves.

The modern dictators do not care much about God. They

want to be gods. Then they can have their own way. Then men become slaves at the beck and nod of one man, a "leader."

When the fear of God goes out, the fear of man takes over.

Secularism knows no God. It deifies the present world. It is without God and without hope in the world.

Read Psalm 90.

Thee God we praise, Thy holy name we bless,
Thee Lord of all, we humbly do confess—
The whole creation ever worships Thee,
The Father of eternity.
The whole creation ever worships Thee,
The Father of eternity.

O Thou most holy, holy, holy Lord,
Thou God of hosts, by all, by all adored;
Earth and the heavens are ever full of Thee,
Thy light, Thy power, Thy majesty.
The earth and heavens are ever full of Thee,
Thy light, Thy power, Thy majesty.

[TE DEUM, adapted]

We Believe in the Works of God

God has spoken (Heb. 1:1-2).
Because that which may be known of God is
manifest to them; for God hath showed it
unto them (Rom. 1:19).

A. WE BELIEVE IN GOD'S REVELATION

If God had not spoken He would be an eternal silence. Then we could not know Him. But as we read in Romans 1: 19 ff.—God has manifested Himself in nature and also in conscience (Rom. 2:14-15). But such revelation could not make known to us a gracious God. So we have a written record of the gradual revelation of God. He revealed Himself according to man's capacity to receive the revelation. Moreover, God's revelation followed a definite plan: *always His own plan of redemption.* God's revelation is based on His foreknowledge of man's fall into sin, and His plan for the salvation of the world. All of God's revelation centers in Christ and His redeeming work with man as the beneficiary. God has spoken, says the Epistle to the Hebrews, and He has spoken in different ways: In times past to the fathers by the prophets—in these last days through His Son (Heb. 1:1 ff.). God has spoken through history, sacred poetry, laws, and He has used the medium of human experience (Wisdom literature of the Old Testament). Both in the Old Testament and in the New Testament God inspired human writers through His Holy Spirit so that we should possess an inerrant record of God's revelation.

THE NECESSITY OF REVELATION

We are aware of the fact that God has revealed Himself both in nature and in conscience. But that revelation is not sufficient for one to come to a full knowledge of the truth, to learn God's way of grace. St. Paul says: "But the natural man receiveth not the things of the Spirit of God: for they are foolishness unto him: neither can he know them, because they are spiritually discerned" (I Cor. 2:14). Natural man can know a God of anger; but the God of love in Christ must be revealed.

Because man was created in the image of God, he has the capacity to receive a supernatural revelation from God. And it is possible for an almighty personal God to reveal Himself to His own creatures.

THE RECORD OF GOD'S REVELATION

Revelation means to make known, to disclose, to unfold. There is a sense in which revelation continues indefinitely. But there is also a sense in which revelation is completed. In its supernatural aspects, and in so far as man's salvation is concerned, the objective revelation is completed. The application of that revelation goes on until the end of time. We believe that in the Bible, the Holy Scriptures, we have a complete and final record of God's revelation. The completion came when Christ appeared. What comes after Christ is the application of God's revelation in the proclamation of God's love in Christ, for the conversion of sinners, for the perfection of the believers.

The Bible is divided into the Old Testament and the New Testament with 39 books in the Old and 27 in the New Testament. Protestants have followed the example of the Palestinian Jews in not accepting the so-called Apocrypha. The Roman Church added the apocryphal (hidden, obscure) books to their Bible as late as the 16th century. (There are 14 so-called apocryphal books.)

The men who wrote the books that now make up the Bible

did not constitute a committee for the purpose of writing a Bible. Over one thousand years elapsed between the writing of the first and the last books of the Bible. *Each book came to be regarded as divinely inspired before the books were collected.* Then there was a collecting process—for the Old Testament completed perhaps at the time of Ezra, approximately 400 B.C. For the New Testament the collecting process was completed about 397 A.D.

Certain definite tests were applied in the collecting process. For the Old Testament: Did the books have the approval of the leaders even before they were collected? Had they been written in Hebrew? *Were they in full harmony with the writings of Moses?* Of the inspiration of the writings of Moses there was no doubt.—As for the New Testament, the books were regarded as divinely inspired long before any collection was made. As the collection came under way the questions asked were the following: Did the particular book have the approval of the early church? Was Christ the center of the narrative? Were the teachings in harmony with the teachings of Christ and the Apostles? Had the books been written by eye- and ear-witnesses to the Lord?

In the case of both the Old Testament and the New Testament historical necessity prompted the collection. In the Old Testament the Babylonian captivity of the Jews hastened the collecting process in order to preserve the Sacred Scriptures. In the New Testament the process was hastened by the death of the Apostles and the rise of many false teachers and spurious books that pretended to have come from apostolic hands.

The Bible then is a collection of many books; written by many men over a long period of time. There is however a remarkable *unity* in the Bible. We discover that the Bible presents to us a History of Salvation. (The German word is *Heilsgeschichte;* in Norwegian, *Frelseshistorie.*) Yes, the whole Bible from beginning to end is the history of God's redemptive plan. It presents the story of a human-divine redeemer, Jesus, the Christ; a way of salvation by faith in that divine redeemer; a people who accepts the way, and who becomes

God's people, in the New Testament the Christian Church. The central theme of the Bible, then, is justification by faith, the story how forgiveness of sin is obtained.

THE INSPIRATION OF THE BIBLE

The Bible does not only contain a more or less completed record of God's dealings with men. It is an inerrant record. It is an inspired record. It is very obvious that the New Testament bears testimony to the inspiration of the Old Testament record. So speaks St. Peter in II Peter 1:21—holy men of God spoke as they were moved by the Spirit of God. So speaks St. Paul in II Timothy 3:16 ff.—The Scriptures are inspired.

But what about the New Testament record? Is that inspired? Certainly. In Galatians 1:11-12 St. Paul writes: "But I certify you, brethren, that the Gospel which was preached of me is not after man. For I neither received it of man, neither was I taught it, but by the revelation of Christ." Then we have a passage in I Thessalonians 2:13 which is equally clear: "For this cause also thank we God without ceasing, because, when ye received the Word of God which ye heard of us, ye received it not as the word of men, but as it is in truth, the Word of God, which effectually worketh also in you that believe." Then it is well to read the entire second chapter of I Corinthians where inspiration is spoken of more fully than anywhere else in the Bible.

No mere external proofs can demonstrate the fact of inspiration. The best proof of inspiration of the Bible is found in the Bible itself: "If any man will do his will, he shall know of the doctrine, whether it be of God, or whether I speak of myself" (John 7:17). "He that believeth on the Son of God hath the witness in himself" (I John 5:10). The power of the Gospel as described in Romans 1:16-17 bears testimony to its divine inspiration. And, of course, the personality of Jesus Christ, the central personality in the whole Bible, bears the most powerful and absolute testimony to the divine inspiration of the Bible. Eternal life is in Jesus, and Jesus is revealed in the Bible (John 5:39, Luke 24:27 and 44, John 8:56, John 5:46-47). The

Word of God is Spirit and life (John 6:63). The Word comes with final authority (John 16:13, II Tim. 3:15).

The fact of divine inspiration is so apparent that we need no particular theory of inspiration. The Bible is the Word of God for it presents the Word which is Jesus Christ, the Son of the living God.

Were we to enumerate the reasons why we believe that the Biblical record is divinely inspired we would say:

1. The Bible presents a God which only a divinely inspired record could present. He is a sovereign God, personal, just, holy, gracious, and a God of love.

2. Sin is presented as a violation of *moral* law: as guilt against God; as separation from God; as needing a God-prepared remedy.

3. The way of salvation is presented as God's effort to reach man. Salvation is by grace alone.

4. The wonderful power of the Gospel.

5. The universality of the message, its timelessness, its eternal youth.

6. The *Christ* of the Bible is absolutely unique. No mere human imagination could produce such a personality. He is in a sense the Bible in so far as we have to get to know Him from the Biblical record. The Bible is the Word of God because it cradles the Christ, as Luther said.

7. The moral code of the Bible is timeless. It must have come from God.

8. The religion of the Bible satisfies man's religious nature.

9. Jesus vouched for the authority of the Old Testament because it was about Him. And the New Testament is also about Jesus, so He vouches for its authority, too.—The Bible is the record of God's inspired revelation, by the content of its own teachings.

Then we have the so-called external evidences:

1. Christian experience verifies the truth of the Bible (John 7:17).
2. Fulfillment of prophecies.
3. The lasting influence of the Bible.
4. Archeology confirms the historical narrative of the Bible.
5. The preservation of the Bible.
6. New discoveries still leave the majestic record of the Bible intact.

The Bible is the Word of God to men. God-inspired men wrote the record. It is profitable for instruction in righteousness. The Words in the Bible are *Spirit* and *Life*. It is dangerous to separate the Word in the Bible from the living Word in the person of Jesus Christ.—Where do we meet Jesus? *In the recorded Word in the Bible.* That was a source of meeting Him even while He was here on earth.—"The Scriptures testify of me," said Jesus (John 5:39). Jesus pointed the doubting disciples to the Scriptures (Luke 24:27, 44). The early disciples of Jesus verified their belief that Jesus of Nazareth was the promised Messiah by turning to the Scriptures: "We have found him, of whom Moses, in the law, and the prophets, did write, Jesus of Nazareth, the son of Joseph" (John 1:45). Likewise we have the testimony of the Apostle Peter in Acts 10:43: "To him give all the prophets witness, that through his name whosoever believeth in him shall receive remission of sin." Yes, and indeed the theme of the whole Bible is *justification by faith*—the remission of sin as a gracious gift of God through Jesus Christ. When one discovers the Christ of the Scriptures then one begins to understand the meaning of the words of the two disciples on the way to Emmaus: "Did not our heart burn within us, while he talked with us by the way, and while he opened to us the Scriptures?" (Luke 24:32). And one of the last testimonies concerning Jesus is this: "Then opened he their understanding, that they might understand the Scriptures" (Luke 24:45).

How Are We to Read the Bible?

Read it prayerfully. Let the Bible explain itself by letting the clearer passages explain the less clear. Read connectedly. Get the setting and the context. Read any one portion of the Bible *in the light of the central theme of the Bible.* Resolve to learn the truth and be guided by it. Let the experience of the church help to throw some light on disputed passages. Assume a literal meaning unless a figurative meaning is clearly indicated.

The Content of God's Word

The Bible contains both Law and Gospel. The Law is to convict of sin, to show the need of Christ, to guide the believer in the path of righteousness. The Gospel, on the other hand, reveals a gracious God (John 3:16). And the Gospel is not a new and improved law. The Gospel is a declaration of God's forgiving love to a penitent sinner, the power of God to save. The Law cannot save. It can only show that we are sinners. "The Gospel gives what the Law demands."

Love is the fulfilling of the Law. When God's love comes into the heart of a penitent and believing sinner, he begins to fulfill the Law. "We love him because he first loved us." Then we love because we are saved by faith, and the keeping of God's Law becomes the fruit of faith—not the means of salvation.

God's Word is absolute and final authority in faith and conduct. That truth is the second, or "Formal," principle of the Reformation.

Read I Corinthians 2 and Luke 24.

> *God's Word is our great heritage,*
> *And shall be ours forever;*
> *To spread its light from age to age*
> *Shall be our chief endeavor;*
> *Through life it guides our way,*
> *In death it is our stay;*
> *Lord, grant, while worlds endure,*
> *We keep its teachings pure,*
> *Throughout all generations.*
> [N. F. S. Grundtvig]

B. WE BELIEVE IN GOD AS CREATOR

> *He spake and it was done; he commanded,*
> *and it stood fast* (Psa. 33:9).
> *Through faith we understand that the worlds*
> *were framed by the word of God, so that*
> *things which are seen were not made of things*
> *that appear* (Heb. 11:3).

God Created Heaven and Earth

In the beginning God created the heavens and the earth (Gen. 1:1).

The Book of Genesis is not essentially an account of *how* God created the earth but it affirms emphatically *that* He created the heavens and the earth, i.e., the universe. Again, Genesis does not fix any date for creation. It says, "In the beginning." And it does not matter to a Christian how old the earth is. What matters is that the earth is the Lord's, that He created it (Ps. 24:1). And He did it by His almighty Word, and He did it as a tri-une God: Father, Son, Holy Spirit.

The earth is not eternal. It had a beginning. God is eternal. He made the universe. It was a free will act on the part of God. The active agent in creation, says the Bible, was the Word. And John calls Jesus the Word.

God did not create anything evil. He allowed "the possibility of situations which would allow sin to appear." There had to be a choice on the part of God's personal creatures. The creation pattern allowed for contrasts, for opposites. We know light because there is also darkness. We know good because there came to be an opposite, evil. Evil is not eternal. It came into being after creation, as far as the world is concerned.

The purpose of creation, as far as God was concerned, was to glorify Himself. The created universe was to show forth God's power, wisdom, goodness, love and infinite majesty. In view of the fact that God placed man upon the earth we can see from the Biblical narrative that He made things for the good of man. For man's use and pleasure God made everything. For Himself He made man. That is why man does not rest until He rests in God. From God, and back to God—that was His plan for man.

God continues to care for His own creation. We believe in God's providence. He permits the created beings to exist as long as they serve His purposes. "He can create and He can destroy." God created; God cares. All things work together for good for those who love the Lord.

In the beginning God. At the end God. The world did not create itself. God called it into being by His almighty Word.

God Created Angels

Are they not all ministering spirits, sent forth to do service for the sake of them that shall inherit salvation? (Heb. 1:14).

Angels are spiritual creatures. Angel worship is expressly forbidden by Paul in his letter to the Colossians.

Angels were created by God to serve Him, to be His messengers, and to render service to Christians. They were present at creation (Job 38:7), at various times in Old Testament history, at the birth of Jesus, etc. In the Old Testament narrative there appears frequently an angel who speaks to certain individuals to reveal God's will.

Angels had to undergo a test, very much like the first people created by God. Some angels revolted, and the chief of them became the devil. When men fell into sin God gave them an opportunity to repent. The angels were given no such chance.

Angels minister to God's believing children. Though we cannot see them we know that their service is real and rendered at God's command.

Believers in Jesus do not become angels when they die. Jesus said: They shall be *like* angels.

God Created Man

And the Lord formed man of the dust of the ground, and breathed into his nostrils the breath of life; and man became a living soul (Gen. 2:7).

Thou madest him a little lower than the angels (Heb. 2:7).

Man has become guilty of both underestimating and over-estimating himself. To make man an animal, even if it be the highest animal, is too low an estimate. To make man the "captain of his soul," the "measure of all things," essentially good, and completely able to guide, direct, and save himself, is too high an estimate.

There are some who have understood the Biblical doctrine of original sin to mean that man is nothing but a worm, worthless and hopeless. That is not the meaning of total depravity. For the doctrine that holds that man is born with a sinful inclination, and that original sin is real sin, does not deny man's abilities in human relationships. It only teaches that he lacks, totally, the power by himself to gain favor with God. But that same teaching which, on the one hand, denies man's ability to either start or complete the saving work in the soul, certainly on the other hand, sees regenerated man elevated to the very presence of God in heaven. So we must guard against misunderstandings and non-Biblical theories.

The Bible teaches that man was created by God in God's own image. That means that man in his spiritual and mental faculties possessed certain likenesses to God. The very fact of man's personality is such a resemblance. Man's free will, before the fall into sin, was part of his personality. He had the power of choice. He is a self-conscious being.

God gave to man a body. That, too, derived benefits from the image of God. But into that body God put a spirit or a living soul. It is customary to say that man's constituent parts are his soul and his body. It is not incorrect to say: body, soul, and spirit (I Thess. 5:23). It all depends on what meaning one puts into the terms used. Sin made man's body mortal. The soul, as we most commonly use that term, is immortal. But the apostle Paul admonishes us to honor God both in our body and our soul, for both belong to God (I Cor. 6:20).

God gave man a free will. The goal of man's will was to choose God—to love Him above all things—and then to regard himself and the world as created by God. The greatest joy of man, therefore, consisted in serving God. All of man's life was to be a life in God and for God. His life was to be God-centered and God-directed.

The tragedy in man's life is his revolt against God, changing his God-dominated life to a self-dominated life. Man's abuse of his free will led him to sin. Man's pride is really the heart of his sin. "You shall be like God," suggested the devil. That created unbelief, pride in man's reason, disobedience. Man, as a free being, sinned. Man, as a personality, had to have the power of choice. Decision is the essence of personality.

But the evil that man chose to follow was not within himself. It came from the outside. One of the good angels, created by God as a free spiritual being, had already revolted against God. That angel became the devil. He made it the object of his existence, from then on, to get man, another creature of God, to revolt against his Maker. Man listened to the enemy of God, yielded to temptation, fell away from God.

Man, as created by God, had all the possibilities to remain in the state in which he came from God. But "as a free moral agent he could choose his path of action."

It is customary to speak of certain stages in man's existence. His first state is called the state of integrity. That was followed by the state of corruption. That gave God the opportunity to establish the state of grace for man. In the state of grace man determines his eternal destiny, whether it shall be a state of misery or a state of glory.

Only in the light of the Word of God does man get his proper place in the universe—created to serve his maker, destined for eternal life (Romans 2:5).

God is the author of life. He created the first human beings. God is also now the author of life. It is possible to explain, biologically, the reproductive processes. But the Christian believes that God works through the laws of life. Thus the creative act now is mediated through the parents of the child. And in view of the doctrine of original sin, it is perhaps the most logical way to accept the theory that a human soul, too, is mediated through the parents. That would explain the strong mental and spiritual resemblances of children to parents. This teaching is known as traducianism.

Read Genesis 1-3.

We all believe in one true God,
Maker of the earth and heaven,
The Father who to us in love
Hath the right of children given;
He both soul and body feedeth,
All we want He doth provide us;
He through snares and perils leadeth,
Watching that no harm betide us;
He cares for us by day and night,
All things are governed by His might.

[M. LUTHER]

We Believe in the Reality of Sin

For all have sinned and come short of the glory of God (Rom. 3:23).
Whosoever committeth sin transgresseth also the law; for sin is the transgression of the law (I John 3:4).

Man has risen quite high in culture and civilization. He has subjected the various laws of nature to his own service. But in all his upward climb a shadow has followed him, a shadow from which he has never been able to run away. To the careful observer the shadow now looks darker than ever since man has overcome so many of the other obstacles on his way in search of happiness. The shadow is sin.

Modern man, as he is by nature, is something like Sisyphus of Greek mythology. In the underworld he was given the job of rolling a stone up a high hill. He did—but every time he came to the top the stone rolled down to the bottom again. According to mythology this will be an eternal job for Sisyphus. This myth illustrates the futility that is in store for those who find no liberating power in life.

The Bible teaches that sin terminated man's fellowship with God. The story of man's fall into sin as told in Genesis is very simple. (1) The woman is willing to enter into conversation with Satan. (2) Doubt and unbelief are expressed concerning the statements made by God. (3) Evil desire and haughtiness appear in her heart. (4) Disobedience results, a deliberate breaking of God's command. Man lost the moral image of God.

God wanted man to be like Him through obedience; the

devil suggested that man should become like God through disobedience. Man was to learn the difference between good and evil. According to God's plan this difference was to be learned through obedience. Man was to abstain from eating the forbidden fruit. The devil wanted man to learn the difference between good and evil by disobeying God, by taking of the fruit of the tree of knowledge.

Sin is lawlessness. It is guilt. It makes man blameworthy before God. Thus, it has broken off man's original relationship with God. Man is by nature no longer right with God.

Sin is therefore not a mere remnant of man's former brutish existence out of which he is gradually evolving himself. The modern optimist would have us believe that sin does not make man guilty before God. Sin is simply a type of weakness, it is said. In due time man will overcome all such remnants of a supposed jungle existence. Such teaching regarding sin is about as shallow as that of certain cults which attempt to solve the sin problem by denying its very existence or by calling it an error in mortal mind. Such teachings square themselves neither with the Bible nor with human experience.

Sin, in its own nature, is made up of two elements: (1) Evil desire or "lust," as the Bible calls it, and (2) Pride.

Man's desire becomes evil when it reaches out to that which is forbidden. Man tries to satisfy himself with that which is in the world rather than with God. Secularism is as old as sinful man. Man makes himself dependent upon the things over which he has been appointed to be Lord. Says the Word: "Love not the world, neither the things that are in the world. If any man love the world, the love of the Father is not in him" (I John 2:15). See also Romans 13:14, Ephesians 2:3, James 1:4 ff, II Peter 1:4. Selfishness enters into the violation of every command given by God.

The First Commandment tells us to have only the one true God. Man was told by Satan that if he did what God had told him not to do, he *would be like God*. So man loves self more than God, trusts self, respects self more than God. He enthrones himself in his own self-made temple.

The Second Commandment tells us not to take God's name in vain. Man will even use God's name, in an oath, to get other people to believe that he is telling the truth when he is actually lying. Sinful man puts self in the center of everything.

The Third Commandment lays down the law of rest. Six days of labor; one of rest. Today many disregard that commandment completely. They never attend divine worship on Sunday. Sunday becomes a day of self-indulgence or a day of continued work in order to gain more for oneself.

The Fourth Commandment demands *obedience* to parents and lawfully constituted authorities. Many people disregard this commandment entirely by saying: I do what I want to do. I do what I like to do, and only what I like to do. Such a philosophy of life leads to the same confusion as in the time of the judges in Israel: Every man did what was good in his own eyes. That kind of behavior results in chaos.

The Fifth Commandment tells about the sacredness of human life. The murderers utterly disregard it. When some one is in their way, kill him; get him out of the way. Hatred in the heart leads to murder.

The Sixth Commandment calls for purity of life whether one is single or married. It forbids divorce. It forbids sexual immorality, sexual promiscuity. Those who break the commandment say: My body is my own. I am entitled to satisfy every demand of the body, to satisfy every lust. I do what I like. The consequences of breaking this commandment show that God's Law cannot be broken without paying the penalty.

The Seventh Commandment sanctions the right to own and use private property. Those who steal violate this commandment. Selfishness shows up here, too. Rather than work for an honest living the thief takes another man's property. Stealing is sin whether the object stolen is small or large. Stealing is usually accompanied by envy and jealousy, but most of all by greed and complete disregard of the rights of other persons.

The Eighth Commandment forbids any kind of false witnessing against our neighbor. People continue to disregard this commandment for selfish reasons. They lie about some one else to build up their own reputation. They pull certain people down by besmirching their character that they may themselves rise higher in the estimation of others. There is gossip and slandering—hurting others to elevate self.

The Ninth and Tenth Commandments forbid *coveting*, evil desires for other people's property, envy and jealousy because others succeed better than themselves. Such envy leads often to false witnessing, some times to murder, always to a life full of tensions, and some times to illness on the part of the person who is envious of others.

Selfishness is at the root of all revolt against God. Men break God's commandments because of selfishness.

According to the Bible sin is now inherent in the human family. So we believe in original sin, inherited sin. Born of a morally tainted race, we are inclined to evil; we are tainted. In myself dwelleth no good thing. Sin lives within me. And original sin is guilt! Sin in the heart soon finds avenues of expression, and we have what we call actual sin, sins of omission and sins of commission.

Sin perverted man's will. Man became the slave of sin (John 8:34). Man's love of truth became perverted. Now man refuses to acknowledge God's truth. Lying is today one of the world's most outstanding sins. Man's conscience is stifled. Man's understanding is darkened. Natural man does not receive the things of the Spirit of God (I Cor. 2:14). See also II Cor. 4:4; Eph. 4:17 ff; Rom. 3:11.

All the world is guilty before God. "The wages of sin is death."

There are many un-Biblical ideas about sin. They vary from the ideas of certain cults which deny the very existence of sin to the modern, so-called *liberal* interpretation, that sin is only a moral weakness. It has also been taught that sin is something attached to the human body. We know from the Scriptures that both devil and sin are realities. We read in I John 3:8— "He that committeth sin is of the devil; for the devil sinneth from the beginning. For this purpose the Son of God was manifested, that He might destroy the works of the devil."

If there is no sin then there is no Savior, and the whole Biblical story is a fraud.

Sin does not reside in the body, but in the will. To be sure, the body had to reap the result of sin in sickness, pain and death. But sin itself is in the will, a will that revolts against God.

Some people, who pretend to follow the Bible, deny its teachings about inherited sin. Many who pay no attention to the Bible also deny this teaching. It is very obvious that the Bible teaches that there is such a thing as inherited sin. Let us call to mind a few Bible passages.

Anyone born of the flesh is flesh (John 3:6). For out of the heart come forth evil thoughts, murders, adulteries, fornications, thefts, false witness, railings (Matt. 15:19). Behold I was brought forth in iniquity; and in sin did my mother conceive me (Ps. 51:5). All have sinned (Rom. 5:12). There is none that doeth good, no not one (Ps. 14:3). And were by nature children of wrath, even as the rest (Eph. 2:3).

We are told that sin brought death into the world. Children die; according to the Bible they have sin. It is not necessary to spend any time at all on teaching children to become self-willed, stubborn, disobedient, etc. And such traits develop even under good environment.

Again we need to note that sin is not merely a reminder that we are on the way up from the slimy deep, and that some day perfection will be reached. No, the sad fact is that sin represents a broken off relationship between man and God. No matter how high we climb the shadow follows us. How does one come to know one self as a sinner? By looking at himself in the light of God's holy Law. It is no use to compare one self with other people. The only comparison that matters is to compare one self with God's demands for perfection. God passes no one with a grade of 70 per cent in keeping His Law. Only 100 per cent is a passing grade with God. That means we all fail. When we see that we begin to understand something about God's grace.

Read Romans 3.

Fast bound in Satan's chains I lay,
Death brooded darkly o'er me,
Sin was my torment night and day,
In sin my mother bore me;
Deeper and deeper still I fell,
Life had become a living hell,
So firmly sin possessed me.

[M. LUTHER]

We Believe in Redemption

> *But when the fulness of the time was come,*
> *God sent forth his Son, born of a woman,*
> *born under the law, to redeem them that were*
> *under the law, that we might receive the*
> *adoption of sons* (Gal. 4:4-5).

A. WE BELIEVE IN JESUS, THE HUMAN-DIVINE SAVIOR

It is not exactly easy to understand the words of the apostle Paul when he says: But the scripture hath concluded all under sin, that the promise by faith of Jesus Christ might be given to them that believe (Gal. 3:22). That every mouth may be stopped, and all the world may become guilty before God (Rom. 3:19).

God foreknew that man would disobey Him. But He decided out of His own mercy and love to save fallen man. God is a sovereign God. He wants humility and obedience in His creatures. Man's sin became the dark background upon which God revealed His atoning love. He hates sin; He loves the sinner. Man's sin could not frustrate God's plan of creation and redemption. Salvation as revealed to man is by pure grace: sinful man cannot earn salvation. God silenced every mouth before Him, declares St. Paul, so that God would have all the glory for saving man. God was moved by His own love to rescue man from sin.

> *Then God beheld my wretched state*
> *With deep commiseration*
> *He thought upon His mercy great,*
> *And willed my soul's salvation.*

He turned to me a father's heart;
Not small the cost! to heal my smart,
He gave His best and dearest.

[M. LUTHER]

When the fullness of time came God sent forth His Son, born of a woman, born under the law (Gal. 4:4), "begotten, not created." He took upon Himself human nature. He was rich, yet for our sakes He became poor, declares the apostle.

So we stand face to face with the mystery of godliness: God was manifest in the flesh, justified in the Spirit, seen of angels, preached unto the Gentiles, believed on in the world, received up into glory (I Tim. 3:16).

According to the Biblical record Jesus claimed to be God. He identified Himself with God. He permitted people to worship Him. It is correct to say that Jesus has *names* ascribed to Him that befit deity: My Lord and my God!—so declared one of His own apostles. God blessed forever (Rom. 9:5). This is the true God and eternal life (I John 5:20). The various *attributes* or qualities ascribed to Jesus are the same as those that belong to God. He is said to be eternal, to have all power, to know all things, to be present wherever two or three are gathered in His name. The *works* He did were the works that God does. He is the medium of creation (John 1:3). In Colossians, St. Paul, in chapter 1, describes Jesus as creator and preserver. Jesus was *worshipped* as only God should be worshipped. Stephen prayed to Jesus (Acts 7:59-60). Believers call on His name (Acts 9:14). The man who had been healed of his blindness worshipped Jesus (John 9:35-38).

Jesus called Himself the Son of Man. Hereby He identified Himself with man, and put Himself above sinful man. By the same title He also claimed Messiahship; for it was by that title the Messiah was made known in the Book of Daniel. He called Himself Son of God. His contemporary Jews said that that was blasphemy and eventually sentenced Him to death because He had made Himself equal with God. Jesus claimed complete oneness with the Father.

Those who heard Him speak afforded Him the honor due

to God. Peter said that He was the Christ, the Son of the living God.

Jesus called Himself David's Son and David's Lord (Matt. 22:42-45). He invited men to believe in God—but in the same statement also to believe in Himself (John 14:1). He pronounces judgment upon the ungodly and tells them to depart from Him (Matt. 25:41). His self-testimony is valid because He was without sin. How could Jesus be part of a sinful race and Himself be perfect, as He claimed He was, unless He also was more than man?

One thing is certain: if Jesus is just another teacher He has no more claim upon me than has a Plato or a Lao-tse. A teacher can only develop what is already in me. But Jesus says that no one can come to the Father but by Him; that He is the Way, the Truth, the Life. He invites men to Himself. (Matt. 11:29). If He were only a teacher, He could only point men to some principle taught, or to a higher power. Jesus spoke with final authority and appealed to no one higher than Himself.

Jesus is not only divine as we are supposed to be divine, as it is affirmed by some students of the life of Jesus. Such students rather freely grant that in the personality of Jesus there is more divinity than in the rest of us. It has been said that the moral character of Jesus perfectly represents the character and purpose of the invisible God. That fact would then entitle Him to be called the Son of God. That does not make Him God, nor even uniquely God's Son. If He is purely a product of the human family, then He must share in the imperfections of the human family. But both He Himself and His followers claimed for Him utter perfection. Evangelical Christians do not only accept the divinity of Jesus, but also the deity of Jesus, God to be worshipped forever. He is one in person with two coordinated natures, the human and the divine. The divine nature was His from eternity; the human nature He assumed. But since He was conceived by the Holy Spirit His human nature was faultless, just as Adam's nature was faultless before he fell into sin. It is for that reason that St. Paul calls Jesus the second Adam, the second representative of the human family.

In the first Adam all men became sinners. In the second, perfect Adam, all men are enabled by faith to gain the righteousness that was His. Yes, Jesus is our divine redeemer. He is the God-man. He is virgin-born. That miraculous birth was in perfect harmony with the supernatural work He had come to perform: to redeem mankind. The God who created the first man continually shows His creative powers. He certainly was the author of that life which resulted in the person of Jesus Christ, the human-divine Savior of the world. To Jesus we address our prayers. He is our Lord and God, one with the Father and the Spirit, God blessed forever.

In the above paragraphs we have stressed the Biblical teaching about the Deity of Jesus; for the tendency today is to deny His Deity, His oneness with God. But stressing His deity does not deny His *humanity*. Said Pilate: Behold the man! Yes, indeed; the perfect man. The man who was the manliest man that ever lived: fearless, courageous, never compromising with evil! Yet tender as a mother, loving, mild, always the friend of publicans and sinners. He loved the little children and had time to visit with them. He put women on the same level as men. He loved the commonplaces of life, and could see the glory of God in the fulfillment of daily tasks. He Himself lived in a unique communion with God, and invited men to communion with God through faith in Him as Savior. Wonderful man! God incarnate!

Read John 1:1-18; Colossians, Chapter 1.

> *Beautiful Savior! King of creation!*
> *Son of God and Son of Man!*
> *Truly I'd love Thee,*
> *Truly I'd serve Thee,*
> *Light of my soul, my joy, my crown!*

B. WE BELIEVE IN THE ATONEMENT

> *And through him to reconcile all things unto*
> *himself, having made peace through the blood*
> *of his cross; through him, I say, whether*
> *things upon the earth, or things in the*
> *heavens* (Col. 1:20).

Yes, as evangelical Christians we believe that Jesus Christ, the God-man, atoned for the sin of the world. We believe that the atonement was substitutionary; He took our place. We believe it was vicarious; He died in our stead. We believe that He made full satisfaction for all our sins, His death was a penalty due to our sins. His death was certainly a demonstration of love for us, but it was equally much the fulfillment of God's just demand upon the sinner. The atonement was an absolute necessity. The whole idea of self-salvation is completely demolished by the Biblical teaching of the atonement, that God was in Christ reconciling the world unto Himself.

The modern tendency is to tone down the absolute necessity of the atonement. Anything in the teaching about the atonement that even hints of an appeasement of an "angry" God brings loud denunciation. God's love is stressed to such a degree that His justice is forgotten. God is made so loving that He never punishes sin upon anybody. His love merely waits for repentance, then it goes into operation in full pardon immediately. It should be remembered that God's justice is just as immutable as His love.

WHAT DOES THE BIBLE TEACH?

St. Paul writes: "Christ hath redeemed us from the curse of the law, being made a curse for us: for it is written, Cursed is every one that hangeth on a tree" (Gal. 3:13). Thus we note that Jesus had to bear man's burden of sin by bearing the curse due to sin. That His work was substitutionary is amply testified by II Cor. 5:21, "For he hath made him to be sin for us, who knew no sin; that we might be made the righteousness of God in him." "And the Lord hath laid on him the iniquity of us all" (Isa. 53:6 b). And again we read in Romans 5:10, "For if, when we were enemies, we were reconciled to God by the death of his Son, much more, being reconciled, we shall be saved by his life."

By His death Christ atoned for our sin; He removed the enmity between us and God and brought reconciliation: "Blotting out the handwriting of ordinances that was against us, which was contrary to us, and took it out of the way, nailing it to the cross" (Col. 1:20). "For Christ is the end of the law for righteousness to every one that believeth" (Rom. 10:4).

Christ entered into your place and mine. He experienced the consequences of sin when upon the cross He felt that He was forsaken of God (Matt. 27:46). The passages regarding this are so numerous that they cannot all be quoted. But for the sake of the reader who wants to find out what the Bible declares on this particular point, the following references give a complete picture of the substitutionary character of the atonement: I Tim. 2:6; Matt. 20:28; Isa. 53:4-5; II Cor. 5:15; I Peter 3:18; John 10:18; I Peter 2:24; John 1:29; Rom. 3:25, 4:25, 5:19; Eph. 1:7; I Peter 1:18-19; Gal. 1:4; I Cor. 15:3; Heb. 10:12, 9:12.

The atonement of Jesus is usually connected with His death upon the cross. By that death Christ took upon Himself the penalty due to sin. That is one side of the atonement. We call it the passive obedience of Jesus. But the law must be kept. And that is the other side of the atonement that Jesus provided for us. He was not only obedient unto death; but He saved us by His life (Rom. 5:10). He said Himself that He had not come to destroy the law and the prophets, but to fulfill (Matt. 5:17). That part of the atonement we call His active obedience.

The work of Jesus is usually discussed under the three headings of Jesus as priest, as prophet, and as king. The atonement or work of reconciliation is His priestly office. Jesus is our priestly mediator. In Him we have the unique situation that priest and sacrifice merge; they become one. That is the reason that Hebrews underscores the "onceness" of the sacrifice of

Jesus: "once for all" (Hebrews 4:14, 7:28, chapter 9). Jesus the last priest!

The prophetic office of Jesus is His teaching office. He did not only point to the Word; He was the Word. In Him the will of God was fully revealed.

The kingly office of Jesus includes His rule over the whole world. But it is particularly in the kingdom of grace that He is king supreme. There will be a kingdom of glory when all the kingdoms of earth shall be His. King of Kings! Lord of Lords!

Thy kingdom come; Thy will be done. His kingdom is righteousness, peace and joy in the Holy Spirit. The citizens in His kingdom are those that He bought with His own blood, and who yield their allegiance to Him.

The atonement of Jesus becomes the ground upon which my personal salvation rests, even as God's love is the source of my salvation, and faith the instrument through which it is acquired. *Without the atonement that Jesus wrought no one could be saved.* It is that important. But the atonement is applied to no one automatically. It has to be accepted. It is a gracious gift of God to fallen man. The sinner who becomes convicted by the Law of God and who takes his refuge in Christ is the only one who begins to sense the deep meaning of the atonement.

The teaching about the atoning sacrifice of Jesus is the heart of the Christian religion. It is the atonement of Jesus that makes Christianity a redemptive religion. The atonement makes Christianity unique. Here God comes to me. "God was in Christ reconciling the world unto Himself." That is the Gospel, the good news. He reconciles me to Himself. He takes the first step. He approaches me. He lives for me; He dies for me. With the apostle Paul we conclude that when He died we died. That is the greatest message the world has ever heard. No wonder the poet exclaims:

> But drops of grief can ne'er repay
> The debt of love I owe.
> Here, Lord, I give myself away
> 'Tis all that I can do.

"He has redeemed me, a lost and condemned creature, bought me and freed me from all sins, from death and the power of the devil; not with silver or gold, but with His holy and precious blood, and with His innocent sufferings and death."—Yes, so said Martin Luther; so say we. The precious blood of Jesus! Revolting, say some. Yes, if they know nothing about a holy God, and a perfect Law, and a just condemnation they may say that. But for the condemned sinner, who knows he is condemned, it is the sweetest story ever told: He died for my sins—"in whom we have redemption, the forgiveness of our sins."

Read Romans 5.

What Thou, my Lord, hast suffered
Was all for sinners' gain;
Mine, mine was the transgression,
But Thine the deadly pain;
Lo, here I fall, my Savior!
'Tis I deserve Thy place;
Look on me with Thy favor,
Vouchsafe to me Thy grace.

[P. GERHARDT]

We Believe in the Person and
Work of the Holy Spirit

> *Cast me not away from thy presence; and*
> *take not thy Holy Spirit from me* (Ps. 51:11).
> *Howbeit when he, the Spirit of truth, is come,*
> *he shall guide you into all truth; for he shall*
> *not speak of himself; but whatsoever he shall*
> *hear, that shall he speak: and he will show*
> *you things to come* (John 16:13).

A. WE BELIEVE IN THE HOLY SPIRIT

WHO IS THE HOLY SPIRIT?

The Holy Spirit is God. He is called God's Spirit. He is
equal with the Father and the Son both in being and in dignity. Jesus calls Him His Spirit. He is named with the other
persons in the Godhead, both in Matt. 28:19-20, and in the
apostolic benediction in II Cor. 13:14. The Scriptures ascribe
to the Holy Spirit divine *names,* as in Acts 5:3-4 where He
is expressly called God. Divine *attributes* are also used in de-
scribing the Holy Spirit. We read in I Cor. 2:10: "For the
Spirit searcheth all things, yea the deep things of God." (See
also John 16:13). The Holy Spirit is described as doing divine
works: "The Spirit of God hath made me, and the breath of
the Almighty hath given me life" (Job 33:4). The Holy Spirit
is also put on an equality with God in being accorded divine
worship. Baptism is performed in His name (Matt. 28:19-20).
The benediction is pronounced in His name (II Cor. 13:14).
He dwells in believers' hearts as His temple (I Cor. 6:19). We

may pray directly to the Holy Spirit. Some of our most precious prayer hymns are addressed to the Spirit.

NAMES USED FOR THE HOLY SPIRIT

The Holy Spirit is called the Spirit of truth, the Comforter (Paraclete), which also means advocate. He is the Spirit of prayer, of wisdom, of power. He is called the Spirit of Christ, the Spirit of God.

THE WORK OF THE HOLY SPIRIT

The work of the Holy Spirit is to apply the fruits of the redeeming work of Jesus to the individual soul. For that purpose He "calls, gathers, enlightens, and sanctifies the whole Christian Church on earth, and preserves it in union with Jesus Christ in the one true faith."

In the sixteenth chapter of John's Gospel the work of the Holy Spirit is indicated. Jesus tells His diciples that when the Comforter comes (in Moffatt's translation He is called the Helper), He will witness concerning Him. The Spirit will convict the world of sin, righteousness, and judgment. The sin is unbelief. The righteousness is that of Jesus Himself which He gained for us by His life, death, and resurrection, the kind of righteousness we need if we are to enter the Kingdom of God. The judgment is the victory of Christ over the devil, a victory in which we share when we are united with Christ.

Without the work of the Holy Spirit we can neither come to Christ nor believe in Him. We, who are dead in trespasses and sin, must be quickened by God's Spirit in His creative and redeeming power.

HOW DOES THE HOLY SPIRIT WORK?

The means through which the Holy Spirit works are the Means of Grace: the Word of God and the Sacraments. That fact explains the difference between the sporadic presence of the Spirit in the Old Testament and the abiding presence in the New Testament Church, beginning with the miracle of Pentecost.

It may be possible to speak about secondary means through which the Spirit works. He prompts us in our conscience. All such promptings are in harmony with God's Word if they are caused by the Spirit. He uses various experiences in life such as illness, perhaps the sudden death of a friend, certain calamities in a community, in order to make us reflect upon our own condition in spiritual matters.

How Do We Get the Spirit of God?

We may answer, first of all, that wherever the Word of God is present, there is God's Spirit. For Jesus says: "The words that I have spoken unto you are spirit, and are life" (John 6:63). Thus, the Spirit is present in baptism because the Word of God is there. Certainly the Spirit is imparted at baptism. Christian baptism is a baptism with water and the Holy Spirit. There is no such thing as a mere water baptism in Christianity.

Then, we are told that the Holy Spirit comes to those who ask for it: "If ye then, being evil, know how to give good gifts unto your children, how much more shall your heavenly Father give the Holy Spirit to them that ask him (Luke 11:13).

The work of the Spirit begins in a human heart to break down man's natural resistance to God. Where the heart is not then willfully closed against the Spirit's influence the good work goes on. In the case of one who by baptism has come into union with Christ the work is one of guidance into assurance and deeper knowledge of God, of daily renewal and growth in holiness and Christian service. In the case of one who has fallen from the grace of God, or who has never experienced God's saving grace, the work of the Spirit comes as a call to repentance and conversion, regeneration, justification, sanctification, assurance and joy. There is an order of salvation. That order we shall consider more fully in later studies.

Read John 16; Acts 2.

Come, Holy Spirit, God and Lord!
Be all Thy graces now out-poured
On each believer's soul and heart;
Thy fervent love to them impart.
Lord, by the brightness of Thy light,
Thou in the faith dost men unite
Of every land and every tongue;
This to Thy praise, O Lord, be sung
Hallelujah! Hallelujah!

[M. Luther]

B. WE BELIEVE IN A CERTAIN ORDER OF SALVATION

For God is not the author of confusion, but
of peace, as in all the churches of the saints
(I Cor. 14:33).
Testifying both to the Jews and also to the
Greeks, repentance toward God, and faith
toward our Lord Jesus Christ (Acts 20:21).
For I shrank not from declaring unto you the
whole counsel of God (Acts 20:27).

We have seen that the Holy Spirit works through the Means of Grace. The purpose is to get man, dead in trespasses and sin, to see his lost condition, to accept God's grace and be saved. Then, the Holy Spirit helps a child of God to grow in grace.

THE AWAKENING AND THE CALL

To awaken a person the Spirit uses the law. "By the law is the knowledge of sin" (Rom. 3:20). Unless a person sees his lost condition, he will not look for help in Christ. So the Spirit of God tries to awaken man's conscience. It is absolutely essential that the law is preached in our churches if there is to be any awakening. When the sinner sees his lost condition, because he has broken God's holy Law, he becomes alarmed. It is then that the Spirit calls him by the Gospel; He invites the sinner to seek God's grace in Christ. It is a gracious call, a loving invitation, a divine illumination.

REPENTANCE–CONVERSION

If the awakened sinner hears and obeys the call, he is moved to repentance. He admits his guilt. He feels sorry that he has offended God. He confesses his sin to God and asks for forgiveness. He believes that God, for the sake of Christ, forgives him all his sins. He resolves, by the grace of God, to shun his former sinful ways. He has felt the power of God who has turned him from his sinful ways to God's way. The sinner has repented and is converted.

REGENERATION–JUSTIFICATION

In the pattern before us we are dealing with a person who has never been in a right relation with God, or one who has fallen away from the grace of God. When such a person is converted—a term used to describe a completed repentance, a turning away from sin, and a turning to God—a change takes place within him. That change is called the new birth. It can be brought about by the Word alone (I Peter 1:23), or by the Word united with the water in baptism (John 3:5). If such a person, awakened by the Law, called by the Gospel, and converted, has never been baptized, he will seek baptism as a sealing and confirming of what God already so graciously has accomplished (Acts 10:44 ff.). For faith and baptism go together (Mark 16:16; Gal. 3:26-27). If he has already been baptized, but has fallen from grace, he will not seek another baptism but rely upon God's gracious will and power to renew the covenant.

This inward change we call the new birth, *regeneration*. As we shall see later, we believe that in the case of infants such birth can be effected by the sacramental Word in baptism, since the spoken Word has no meaning to the infant, yet he is in need of God's regenerating power because of inherited sin. For the adult it is a change of attitude, and insight, direction, and motivation. The Holy Spirit brings about a hatred of sin, a love for God, His Word, and His people. The will is changed so it wills to do good. Love to God becomes the new motive power in living. The mind is enlightened by the Holy Spirit so that it gets a quickened insight into the meaning of God's Word. The Spirit testifies in the heart to the actuality of the new life (Rom. 8:16).

Simultaneously with this change within there is a change of relationship between the sinner and God. The repentant sinner becomes a saved sinner, a forgiven, an acquitted sinner. That change of status we call justification. It is brought about by the faith that looked to Christ as its only hope, the faith that received the pardon so freely offered by Christ. Justification takes place just as soon as faith grasps God's grace. So that Faith, regeneration, justification all function in the same moment.

Justification is an imputation of divine grace. Romans 4 uses that word or its equivalent no less than eleven times. God reckons to the penitent and believing sinner all that Christ did for the sinner. God forgives him, declares him free, looks upon the sinner through His Son, and accepts the believing sinner into sonship with Himself as if he had done all that Jesus did. One died; all died. The sinner is now a child of God. The source of justification is God's love; the ground upon which God forgives is the atonement wrought by Christ; the instrument provided by God for the acceptance of this gift is faith. And this saving faith is essentially trust, confidence, full reliance upon the grace of God, receptivity. It will issue in a new obedience. But since the Gospel is not a new Law, but a gift of God, faith is essentially that God-given quality in a man's soul by which he receives what God offers in the Gospel.

The man who was dead in trespasses and sin could not by his own powers assist in his conversion. But when he quit opposing God's call, when he stopped refusing God's gracious invitation, then God could save him. However, as soon as a man has thus experienced God's saving grace, he is enabled to work together with God's Spirit in his own development.

SANCTIFICATION

Sanctification is the name for the process that begins in the heart and life of the saved man. Sanctification is the name for the growing Christian life. There can be no sanctification without justification. Good works, as fruits of faith, are possible only in the life of the believer. The unbeliever may in his civic life do much "good." But his good deeds are not the fruits of faith and therefore not a part of a Christian sanctifying process.

Sanctification is fostered by the use of God's Word and the Lord's Supper. Prayer is a means by which God gains access to the soul with the blessings in His Word. The Christian lives in the atmosphere of prayer. For his spiritual exercise the Christian person finds himself engaged in Christian service of many types: Teaching, visiting the sick, inviting people to church, doing mission work in various ways—witnessing unto Jesus in all that he says, in what he is and in what he does. Sanctification is many-sided; since human nature is with us all through life, sanctification is a life-long process. (See Philippians 3.) Public worship is an essential part of sanctification, as well as stewardship of one's time, talents, and money.

GLORIFICATION

Glorification, ultimate vision of God, is the goal of sanctification. Though salvation is for the here and now its ultimate goal is life with God in heaven. In "playing the game of life" it is well to remember the goal.

In the whole process of bringing a person to God we note that the grace of God is needed all the way. He who most fully learns to appropriate God's grace lives the fullest Christian life; for in loving and thankful service he wants to honor God who saved the sinner by grace, and who by grace maintains him on the way through life. With God there is all the grace needed both for living and for dying.

WHAT ABOUT PREDESTINATION?

"The doctrine about predestination must always be interpreted in the light of the whole gracious plan of God to save men by the atoning blood of Christ, and that men by faith appropriate the benefit of that sacrifice. Predestination does not stand alone. It is not arbitrary. It is part of God's great and gracious plan for the salvation of sinners. It must not be separated from the teaching about justification by faith. In Christ we are justified, i.e., forgiven; in Christ we are predestined. The determining factor, then, is our relationship to Christ. God's whole order of salvation is indeed an election on His part; for by grace we are saved. The order given in the letter to the Ephesians is the following:

"1. God's eternal counsel and decision to save mankind.

"2. The realization of this eternal plan of God in time—when Christ came (Eph. 1:4-7 a).

"3. The proclamation of the salvation which God had prepared and made known (Eph. 1:7 b-10).

"4. Those who in faith accept Christ are made partakers of the blessed salvation which God in Christ so freely provided (Eph. 1:11-14).

Thus the whole plan of salvation honors God who made it possible. God must therefore be praised for His abundant grace." *

We are elected in Christ. God knew that Man would fall into sin. He decided to provide a means of escape by sending His Son to the world. His foreknowledge clearly enters into His predestination. Those that He knew would accept Jesus Christ He predestined. If we are saved, the glory belongs to God who made our salvation possible. If we are lost, the responsibility is ours.

What about those who did not have any opportunity of choice? We have only one answer: God condemns no one unjustly.

But what about predestination and man's responsibility? That question can best be answered by putting the two together and finding God's bridge between them.

---

*Your Key to the Bible—page 153.

The Sovereignty of God

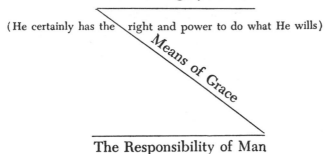

(He certainly has the right and power to do what He wills)

Means of Grace

The Responsibility of Man

The Means of Grace are available. Man can will to expose himself to God's Word and the preaching of it. Thus we see that the Means of Grace, God-provided, form the bridge between God's sovereign power and man's responsibility in deciding what to do with God's gracious plan.

When it is remembered that to God alone belongs the glory for our salvation, it is correct to follow Dr. H. E. Jacobs in his presentation of the problem of election:

Paul was { justified / elected } { in view / of } { the merits of Christ accepted by faith }

The cause of justification is the same as the cause of election: God's great love. The ground of both justification and election is the atonement of Jesus. God's election, to be effective, must be appropriated. And faith is the instrument of appropriation.

WHAT THEN SHALL I DO TO BE SAVED?

Repent and believe the Gospel. Confess your sins to God. Accept the Lord Jesus Christ and the forgiveness He provided. Says the apostle Paul: For ye are all the children of God by faith in Christ Jesus. For as many of you as have been baptized into Christ have put on Christ (Gal. 3:26-27). Those who remain in the true faith until the end are saved, are predestined. Saved now; remain in the faith; saved forever.

CAN I BE CERTAIN OF MY SALVATION?

That was indeed one of Luther's great discoveries that certainty of salvation and the joy of salvation can and *must* be ours. Such certainty rests upon the *completed* work of Jesus for our salvation. It is finished! He said. Faith accepts the completed salvation and enters into possession of it. That ends uncertainty. This faith rests on the promises of God, and can be joyful and secure only as long as it abides in Christ. It does not rest upon feelings and emotions. They vary. The Word of God never changes. To the Word I must constantly return if I am to have a true certainty of my salvation.

How do I know that I am a child of God? The apostle Paul has a very significant answer in Rom. 8:14. "For as many as are led by the Spirit of God, they are the sons of God." Also in verse 16 of the same chapter: "The Spirit itself beareth witness with our spirit, that we are the children of God." We call that the testimony of the Spirit.

The daily life of the Christian also becomes a testimony to the reality of a changed life, or of a life that has continually been in harmony with the will of God by daily repentance and faith.

Read Eph. 1; Romans 8.

> *Blessed Savior, who hast taught me*
> *I should live to Thee alone;*
> *All these years Thy hand hath brought me*
> *Since I first was made Thine own.*
> *At the font my vows were spoken*
> *By my parents in the Lord,*
> *That my vows shall be unbroken,*
> *At the altar I record.*

I would trust in Thy protecting,
Wholly rest upon Thine arm;
Follow wholly Thy directing,
O my only guard from harm!
Meet me now with Thy salvation,
In the Church's ordered way;
Let me feel Thy confirmation
In Thy truth and fear today.

So that, might and firmness gaining,
Hope in danger, joy in grief,
Now and evermore remaining
Steadfast in the true belief;
Resting in my Savior's merit,
Strengthened, with the Spirit's strength,
With Thy Church I may inherit
All my Father's joy at length.

[J. M. NEALE]

C. WE BELIEVE IN THE MEANS OF GRACE

And they continued steadfastly in the apostles'
doctrine and fellowship, and in breaking of
bread, and in prayers (Acts 2:42).
So then faith cometh by hearing, and hearing
by the Word of God (Rom. 10:17).
And now why tarriest thou? Arise, and be
baptized, and wash away thy sins, calling on
the name of the Lord (Acts 22:16).

1. THE CHIEF MEANS OF GRACE IS THE WORD OF GOD

It is a pronounced feature of Lutheran theology that it
teaches that God's Holy Spirit works through certain means.
The Means of Grace, as commonly defined, are said to be the
Word of God and the Holy Sacraments. These means are
sometimes called primary. It is then customary to list as sec-

ondary means the Church, the ministry in the Church, the State, the home, and the family.

Lutheran theologians have not favored the inclusion of prayer in the enumeration of the Means of Grace. It is to be noted that in a recent dogmatical work by Dr. Aulen of Sweden, prayer is called a Means of Grace. Of course, it all depends on what one puts into the use of certain terms. Now, it happens that most of us have looked upon the Means of Grace as channels or vehicles through which God makes His grace available to us. Prayer, on the other hand, has been looked upon as our approach to God. There can be nothing radically wrong in calling prayer a Means of Grace if we assume that it helps us to be put in such a relationship to God that we become receptive to the grace that flows through His Word to us.

The chief Means of Grace is the Word of God. Indeed Luther looked upon the Word as the chief *sacrament,* which in reality it is. *The sacrament of the Word!* In the Word God speaks to us. In the sacraments God acts upon us.

God has seen fit to approach us through the Means of Grace in order to give us the opportunity of choice. He does not force His grace upon us. God offers His grace. Man accepts or rejects.

We have already spoken about the inspired Word of God in the Bible. We have inferred why it becomes a Means of Grace. The Word of God in the Bible is not dead. *The word of God is quick, and powerful, and sharper than any two-edged sword, piercing even to the dividing asunder of soul and spirit, and of the joints and marrow, and is a discerner of the thoughts and intents of the heart* (Heb. 4:12).

No dead letter, as the Quakers teach, and who wait for the "inner light." God's Law reveals sin, and pronounces judgment upon the sinner. God's Gospel invites the sinner to seek the grace of God. And God's Word has the power to confer that to which it invites men. The question is: "Believest thou the Gospel?" If the answer is "yes" then the Gospel brings the assurance of forgiveness. And where there is forgiveness, as

Luther says, there is life and salvation.—"They that gladly received the word were baptized" (Acts 2:41). Hearing is by the Word, says the apostle Paul.—It is necessary that we come under the influence of the Word of God. Our ultimate destiny will be determined by our relation to the Word: "The word that I have spoken, the same shall judge him in the last day" (John 12:48). Power to save; power to judge.

Said Jesus: It is the spirit that quickeneth; the flesh profiteth nothing: the words that I speak unto you are spirit, and they are life! (John 6:63).

The Word of God, as we have seen, is made up of both Law and Gospel. The whole Word of God functions to make it a means of Grace. The Law works on the conscience to convict of sin. It becomes like a mirror to reveal to ourselves how sinful we are. That makes us look for a remedy. But the Law can no more cleanse from sin than the mirror can cleanse our face from grime. So we learn from the Gospel about the love of God in Christ and hear God's gracious invitation.—It is through the reading of the Word or the hearing of it or remembering it, if we once learned it, that we are led to repentance and faith. It is a Means of Grace because it brings us into contact with the God of all grace, revealed in Jesus Christ. It is the Means of Grace because through it our spiritual life is nourished, our life directed, our faith strengthened. It keeps us in contact with God.

> Lamp of our feet, whereby we trace
> Our path, when wont to stray,
> Stream from the fount of heavenly grace,
> Brook by the travelers' way;
>
> Bread of our souls, whereon we feed,
> True manna from on high;
> Our guide and chart, wherein we read
> Of realms beyond the sky;
>
> Pillar of fire through watches dark,
> Or radiant cloud by day;
> When waves would 'whelm our tossing bark,
> Our anchor and our stay:

Word of the ever-living God,
Will of His glorious Son;
Without Thee how could earth be trod,
Or heaven itself be won?

Lord grant us all aright to learn
The wisdom it imparts;
And to its heavenly teachings turn,
With simple, childlike hearts.

[B. BARTON]

2. WE BELIEVE IN SACRAMENTAL GRACE

"The like figure whereunto even baptism doth now save us"
(I Peter 3:21).
"Unto the remission of sins" (Matt. 26:36).

Long ago someone made the following comparison of the various church groups as we know them today: The Roman Church puts the emphasis on the *sacraments*. There are in the Roman Church seven sacraments, and when they are duly administered by bishop or priests they function as it were by themselves. (Baptism, in emergency, may be administered by a lay person.) The reformed churches put the emphasis upon the *Word*. To them the sacraments are essentially emblems and symbols. One Baptist theologian in a recent publication stated: "But in this ordinance [The Lord's Supper], as in that of baptism, it is necessary to adhere simply to the fact that they are symbols. There is no spiritual grace conferred in either" *(The Christ of the Gospels,* J. W. Shepard, p. 544).

The Lutheran position is that both *Word and sacrament* must be emphasized. That designation is, from the Lutheran point of view, correct, because it views the sacraments in the light of the Word. There is something that may be called the "sacramental Word." It is still the Word of God; but it is the Word connected with visible means in an institution ordained by Christ Himself.

Therefore, he who belittles the sacraments belittles both Christ and the Word. Again, the very fact that the sacraments are dependent upon the Word makes it impossible for them to work "by themselves" *(ex opere operato)*. There must be a willingness on the part of the participant to receive grace. The one who administers the sacrament can neither add to nor detract from the actual, inherent efficacy of the sacrament. The Word fixes the value of the sacrament. The individual determines whether the inherent value of the sacrament will be his. In Luther's explanation of baptism, he says ". . . but the Word of God connected with the water, and our faith which relies on that word. For without the Word of God, it is simply water and no baptism"—the Word, and faith which trusts the Word.

There is thus in the sacraments an inter-communion, an inter-action, between man and God. It is God who helps to create the very faith that in turn reaches up to Him. Here even the helpless infant can be touched by the divine. The spoken Word, in the case of the infant, cannot take effect; the "sacramental Word" can reach because in the child there is no resistance to that boundless grace of God which surrounds us from our infancy.

FAULTY EVALUATION

Why do men belittle the divine institutions of the sacraments? That is difficult to understand. Historically the Reformed attitude came as a reaction to Romanism with its almost magical concept of the sacraments. If one wonders at the underestimation of the sacraments, one may be equally concerned with the over-estimation of them, which is also dangerous. In most cases where we find an overestimation we usually find it attached to priest-craft in one form or the other. And priest-craft leads to work-righteousness, and detraction from the grace of God. Where the sacraments become magical formulas, the human agent becomes too important and the recipient tends to free himself from personal responsibility. Even the good gifts of God are subject to human abuse as we see so clearly in the history of church and dogma.

It is interesting to note that where the sacraments are underestimated, contrary to common belief, the grace of God is also frequently underestimated. Salvation becomes something I help to achieve by a particular kind of conversion. It can easily become a form of legalism where one insists upon just one particular way of approaching God. How we need to guard against extremes!

Read II Timothy 3; Acts 20.

Open mine eyes, O Lord,
Open mine eyes.
Thy Word and Sacraments
Let me ne'er despise!
Thou art the Way, O Lord;
Thou art the Truth, O Lord;
Thou art the Life, O Lord;
Open mine eyes.

[CLARENCE A. JOHNSON]

We Believe in the Sacrament of Baptism

> And Jesus came and spoke unto them, saying:
> All power is given unto me, in heaven and
> in earth. Go ye therefore, and make disciples
> of all nations, baptizing them into the name
> of the Father, and of the Son, and of the Holy
> Ghost; teaching them to observe all things
> whatsoever I have commanded you; and, lo, I
> am with you always even unto the end of
> the world (Matt. 28:18-20).
> He that believeth and is baptized shall be
> saved; but he that believeth not shall be con-
> demned (Mark 16:16).

Evangelical Christianity recognizes two sacraments: Baptism and the Lord's Supper. Our word sacrament is derived from the Latin *sacramentum*, a sacred thing, an oath of allegiance, a pledge made by parties in a law case. The Greek word is *mysterion*. Protestants accept only two sacraments, for in the New Testament there are only two ordinances that are (1) divinely instituted as observances to be perpetuated (so also in the early church); (2) and having visible means, earthly elements (water in baptism; bread and wine in the Lord's Supper); (3) and the promise attached concerning the available heavenly grace in the ordinances.

Even in the oral gospel, which preceded the written, baptism unto remission of sin was a definite part. "The washing [laver] of regeneration" it is called by St. Paul (Titus 3:5). "Birth of water and the Spirit" it is named in John 3. And, as for the Lord's Supper, we read: "Given and shed for you for the remission of sin." The two sacraments correspond very closely to the whole concept of the Christian life: its beginning and its maintenance. Baptism is at the beginning. The Lord's Supper is the ordinance of renewal, sanctification.

The two sacraments of the Christian Church correspond very closely to the ordinances in the Old Testament of circumcision and the Passover. The first named ordinance was the sign of the covenant God made between Himself and Israel. It dates back to Abraham. To bring a spiritual blessing to the individual it was to show itself effective in pious living. As a rite it was to remind the pious Israelite of his covenant relationship with God.

The Passover was essentially a reminder of the fact that God keeps His covenant. He remembers His people. He delivers them from oppression. He who saves from the slavery of Egypt also saves from the more serious slavery of sin. For that deliverance the Lamb of God Himself must come to the world.

CHRISTIAN BAPTISM WAS INSTITUTED BY JESUS

Baptism was instituted by Jesus, i.e., Christian baptism. Before He gave us our baptism we hear about John's baptism which was unto repentance for those who confessed their sins (Matthew 3). But John's baptism was not meant to be a New Testament ordinance, which is clearly seen from Acts 19. People who had received John's baptism were baptized in the name of Jesus by St. Paul. John's baptism with water was not sufficient.

To base any argument for or against any phase of Christian baptism on John's baptism is futile. There is nothing at all in the incident of the baptism of Jesus by John that relates to either age or mode in Christian baptism.

Jesus Himself gives the reason for requesting John to baptize Him: "To fulfill all righteousness." Of course that means that the baptism of Jesus by John was part of the plan of salvation that Jesus was to carry out. John's baptism was unto repentance for those who confessed their sin. Jesus had no sin of His own. But He was the Lamb of God who carried the sin-burden of the whole world. So His baptism was one in which He officially and publicly identified Himself with the sinful human family, as the second Adam, to deliver us from sin. A baptism of identification, then. It was a baptism that became for Jesus the inaugural for His public ministry. It is also here very interesting to note that even as Jesus identified Himself with us by His baptism, so we are to identify ourselves with Him by our baptism. (Buried with Him by baptism unto death—baptized into Christ, put on Christ.)

Furthermore if John's baptism had anything to do with Christian baptism, then why did Jesus institute baptism at the close of His ministry here on earth? The baptism of Jesus Himself, by John, has a great deal to do with the redemptive plan of God; but it has nothing to do with our own baptism as such.

We next observe that Jesus instituted baptism with no differentiation between adult or infant baptism at all. He gave us baptism, a baptism unto discipleship. All nations! Make them my disciples by baptizing them and by teaching them. These two cannot be separated. They are so closely knit together, according to the rule of the language used, that there can hardly be the one without the other.

Again we observe that baptism never stands alone. It is always connected with the whole Christian life, particularly with the beginning of the Christian life, the admittance into the church, the adoption into God's family. But all beginnings have significance for future development. So with baptism.

WHAT IS BAPTISM?

The answer has just been given from Matthew 28:19-20. Baptism is the door into discipleship with Jesus. It thus becomes the door into the Christian Church; for disciples of Jesus constitute the church. According to Titus 3:5 baptism is the washing of regeneration. According to I Peter 3:21 it has the same effect as Noah's ark which saved Noah's household from the flood. Says Peter: "The like figure [like the ark] whereunto even baptism doth also now save us" (I Peter 3:23a).

In defining baptism it is difficult to separate what it is from what it does. "He who believes and is baptized shall be saved; but he that does not believe shall be condemned" (Mark 16:16). The New Testament definitely connects baptism with salvation. Because it connects baptism with Christ; with repentance; with adoption; with faith; with forgiveness; with regeneration; with the impartation of the Holy Spirit. What is baptism? It is the ordinance that connects us with Jesus. (1) Baptized into the name of the Tri-une God (Matt. 28). (2) Sons of God by faith in Christ—"because as many of you as have been baptized into Christ have put on Christ"—"that we might receive the adoption of sons" (Gal. 3:26-27, and 4:5). Into the name of: that makes us part of God's family.

Baptism is connected with repentance. "Repent and be baptized every one of you in the name of Jesus Christ for the remission of sins, and ye shall receive the Holy Ghost" (Acts 2:18). Also note that in this verse we see clearly that baptism is associated with Christ, repentance, forgiveness, and the granting of the Holy Spirit. To Saul of Tarsus it was said: "And now why tarriest thou? Arise, and be baptized, and wash away thy sins, calling on the name of the Lord" (Acts 22:16).

Baptism is more than an "outward sign of an inward change." Because the Word is added to the water according to the command of Jesus, the baptismal Word can bring about a *change*. The statements in John 3 about the new birth have been recognized from the earliest times to refer to baptism. To be born of water and the Spirit (John 3:5) must refer to baptism as one may infer from Ephesians 5:26: That He might sanctify and cleanse it (the church) with the washing of water by the Word. What kind of washing of water by the Word could be found in the early church except baptism? None.

It is interesting to note a modern Methodist scholar accepting the above named interpretation of John 3 (W. F. Howard: *Christianity According to St. John*).

The validity of baptism is found in the fact that it is instituted by Jesus Christ and that it connects a person with Christ. Jesus Christ is our Savior; baptism connects us with Jesus, through faith.

WHAT IS THE PROPER MODE?

How should one be baptized? Lutherans have no quarrels with anybody about the mode of baptism except where the mode is made so important that only one particular way is acceptable. The very word *baptize* means to dip into water, to wash with water, to sprinkle with water, to pour water upon, to immerse in water. That the word baptize cannot always mean to immerse in water is clearly seen from Mark 7 where it is stated that tables were washed. The word in the original is to baptize. Baptizing tables must mean to wash tables. They were not immersed. Baptism by sprinkling is as valid as by immersion.

WHAT BENEFITS ARE CONFERRED BY BAPTISM?

We have already answered that question. But for the sake of clarity let us enumerate the benefits as we find them in the Bible. On the basis of Mark 16:16 Dr. Martin Luther says in his Catechism of 1529: "Baptism works forgiveness of sin, delivers from death and the devil, and gives everlasting salvation to all who believe, as the Word and promise of God declare. Where there is forgiveness, there is life and salvation."

St. Peter declares that the Word regenerates (I Peter 1:23). But he never denies the regenerating power of that same Word when attached to baptism. He rather affirms it in I Peter 3:21 where he gives the same saving power to baptism as Noah's ark had for the people who were saved from the flood.

We have seen that Biblical, Christian baptism is connected with discipleship, forgiveness, repentance, faith, adoption, regeneration, granting of the Holy Spirit—therefore with salvation because it connects one with Jesus. Jesus lived and died for our salvation. Baptism brings us into fellowship with Him.

Do these benefits come to one automatically or by the mere application of baptism? No. The recipient has to be receptive, which is the same as saying that he must have faith in the Word, faith in Christ.

WHO SHOULD BE BAPTIZED?

All who want to be disciples of Jesus. All who want to be adopted into God's family (into the name of; baptized into Christ). All who want to be saved. All who seek the gift of regeneration. All who want to identify themselves with Christ and His church. If conversion precedes baptism, in the case of an adult, by the hearing of God's Word, such a convert will immediately seek the sealing grace of God, for such a conversion, in baptism. This is the Biblical order for adults.

How Can These Stipulations Be Applied to Children?

Quite easily if one is willing to follow God's Word rather than one's own rationalizing.

1. Salvation, as provided by God, does not work automatically. It has to be mediated; it has to be accepted. To say that children are "under the blood" up to a certain age without doing anything for them is totally unwarranted by the Bible. He who does not believe shall be condemned (Mark 16:16). Without faith it is impossible to please God (Heb. 11:6). So if infants can have no faith there is no salvation for them. For the Word makes no exception to either sinfulness or the need of salvation for any age group.

2. Infants need God's grace, for they are part of a sinful race. John 3: *Anyone* born of flesh is flesh. Romans 5: Wherefore as by one man sin entered into the world, and death by sin; and so death passed upon all men, for that *all* have sinned. Psalm 51: Conceived in sin, born in iniquity. Ephesians 2: By nature the children of wrath even as others.—The wages of sin is death. *Children die;* they must have sin. We do not have to teach children disobedience and stubbornness. They are disobedient and stubborn before they learn from others.

3. Infants can be reached by God's grace through the ordinance of baptism. We are to disciple all nations! (Matt. 28.) The promise is to you and your children (Acts 2:39). Permit the little children [infants] to come unto me (Mark 10:14); to them belongs the kingdom of God.—But by their natural birth they are not in God's kingdom (John 3:6). They must be born of water and the Spirit (John 3:5). They can enter God's kingdom through God's appointed means: baptize, teach. They can enter God's kingdom; for Jesus told adults that adults cannot enter the kingdom unless they turn and become like children (Mark 10:15; Matt. 18:3). By grace are ye saved, we are told in Ephesians, it is the gift of God (Eph. 2:8). If salvation is a gift by grace then age cannot earn it; neither can reason nor knowledge. Only a receptive heart can receive His gift.

4. Infants can have such a saving faith. In the first place Jesus so declared in Matt. 18:6—these little ones who believe in me. And "little ones" means little children, babies. Believe in Jesus means to trust in Him, to be receptive to His grace. Infants do not resist the grace of God. Therefore they can receive it through God's appointed means: Make disciples by baptizing and teaching.

5. Infants cannot be reached by the spoken Word, so we believe they can be reached by the sacramental Word. Would God make no provision for the children in the New Testament when He so amply provided for the children in the Old Testament covenant? In Col. 2:11 ff., we see that New Testament baptism is compared with Old Testament circumcision. God could and God can make a covenant with children; for it is a covenant of grace. Children who are within the household of the faith should be baptized, and they must be taught.

Opponents of infant baptism say: Show me where, in the New Testament, infant baptism is commanded. It is equally proper to say: Show me where it is forbidden. All nations include children. *And if children are not included, then how long are they too good to be condemned? and when are they old enough to be saved?*

6. The apostolic church baptized infants. So declares Origen, an early Alexandrian Christian teacher. Tertullian of North Africa questioned infant baptism. Not because it was not used; but because he doubted God's ability to do anything for infants. The New Testament reports the baptism of whole families without ever referring to age: Acts 10; Acts 16; Acts 18:8; I Cor. 1:16.

7. Children are regarded as citizens by birth even without knowledge. Children can possess property before they know that they possess it. I can *give* a child a sum of money, put it in the bank in the child's name, and the money belongs to the child. Children can be legally adopted without their knowledge. God can also graciously adopt them (Gal. 3:26-27 and 4:5-7). Baptism confers grace; it is a gift of God. It can be possessed by a child. Then the child must be taught, nurtured in the Christian faith, brought to God in prayer. Then such a child must come to a personal awareness of his relationship to God, a conscious decision to follow Christ. Should such a child stray from God then there must be a genuine conversion, a return to the Father's home, if such a person is to be saved.

Some of the greatest leaders of the Church of Christ were baptized in their infancy: Luther, Calvin, Wesley. They had God's Spirit. We have seen how God's Spirit came through baptism (Acts 2:38-39).

If one really believes in original sin, and that salvation is a work of God, by grace only, a pure gift, then it is easy to understand infant baptism.

IS BAPTISM NECESSARY?

Yes. But where God binds us He does not necessarily bind Himself. Discipleship is through baptizing and teaching. But the penitent thief on the cross was likely not baptized. He was saved. He was regenerated by the Word. But again that does not eliminate regeneration by the Word as connected with baptism. The case of the thief on the cross is an unusual one.

We determine a Christian doctrine by the ordinary and usual, not by the unusual and extraordinary.

WHAT ABOUT BAPTISMAL REGENERATION?

By non-Lutherans, in the Protestant family of churches, that doctrine is condemned. Lutherans believe in it on the basis of John 3 and Titus 3:5 and I Peter 3:21 ff.; Eph. 5:26. The early church held that belief.

The baptized child can remain in its baptismal covenant if it is properly instructed and guided by Christian parents, pastors and teachers. God certainly can keep His promise. But as grace can be resisted, so one can fall away from grace, and such a one must be restored. God, who never breaks His covenant, is willing to receive the repentant sinner. Thus baptism plays an important part in the whole religious life of a child. St. Augustine said: "If I had been baptized as an infant I would have been spared from many of the sins of my youth."

The one who has been baptized can say: "Dear Father, thou didst adopt me. Please keep me; please make me willing to be kept." The one who may have fallen away can say: "Please, Father, renew with me the blessed covenant of my baptism." Of course, every Christian needs such a daily renewal.

HOW SHALL WE PROCEED?

If we are dealing with unchurched people, whether on the foreign field or here at home, we must begin by evangelizing them, teaching them the Law and the Gospel. Then if by God's Spirit through the Word, they are moved to accept the Lord we baptize them. "Then they that gladly received his word were baptized; and the same day there were added to the church about three thousand souls" (Acts 2:41).

Then when a household of the faith has been established, a covenant people of God, a Christian congregation, then we can apply the analogy of faith—take all the passages of God's plan in their proper connection and apply them. Now we have the assurance of compliance with Christ's commission. Now we can include little children; for God's promise is to them, too (Acts 2:39). Children are never excluded from any of God's promises except where self-examination is made a condition for participating in the Lord's Supper (I Cor. 11:28): They cannot examine themselves. Otherwise God deals with whole families, as we have seen, without any age limitations.

God's plan was to include all nations into His covenant people. Individuals and nations have revolted against God. The church must try to win them for Christ by proclaiming the Gospel. The proclamation of the Gospel and baptism go hand in hand.

Read Acts 2; Acts 16; Acts 22.

He that believes and is baptized
Shall see the Lord's salvation;
Baptized into the death of Christ,
He is a new creation;
Through Christ's redemption he shall stand
Among the glorious heavenly band
Of every tribe and nation.

With one accord, O God, we pray:
Grant us Thy Holy Spirit;
Look Thou on our infirmity
Through Jesus' blood and merit!
Grant us to grow in grace each day
By holy baptism that we may
Eternal life inherit!

[T. KINGO]

We Believe in the Lord's Supper

> *Words of Institution:* Matt. 26:26-28; Mark 14:22-24; Luke 22:19-20; I Cor. 11:23-25.
> *The cup of blessing which we bless, is it not the communion of the blood of Christ? The bread which we break, is it not the communion of the body of Christ?* (I Cor. 10:16).

Baptism is the sacrament of entrance into the Church and the kingdom of God. The Lord's Supper is the sacrament of renewal, of sanctification. It must never be forgotten that baptism is not something that has such a "oneness" about it that it plays no part in a person's life after its initial use. It should mean a great deal in our daily Christian experience. Though the sacrament of baptism itself is not renewed, the baptismal covenant should be renewed daily. For baptism is a covenant (I Peter 3:21). If the covenant is to be effective, one must live up to the terms of the contract: renunciation of evil, and faith in the Triune God. Putting off the "old man"; putting on the "new man" after the image of God.

CONFIRMATION

Confirmation is not a sacrament, but a rite in the Church. It grows out of the Great Commission: "baptize . . . teach." It is part of the very life of the Church. For the Christian life is connected with teaching the precepts of Christianity. Instruction has been part of God's plan for His people both in the Old Testament and the New. Then comes the personal appropriation of what one has been taught, and a personal confession. Says the apostle Paul: "The word is nigh thee, even in thy mouth, and in thy heart: that is, the word of faith, which we preach; that if thou shalt confess with thy mouth the Lord Jesus, and shalt believe in thy heart that God hath raised him from the dead, thou shalt be saved. For with the heart man believeth unto righteousness; and with the mouth confession is made unto salvation" (Romans 10:8-10). Those are the Biblical foundations for the rite of confirmation. Historically, confirmation is a continuation of the early catechumenate in the Church, the class in preparation for entrance into the Church.

Confirmation is instruction in the Word of God and a confession of one's faith. In as far as it is instruction and a personal confession, it becomes a renewal of the baptismal covenant. But again, the rite of confirmation is not characterized by its "onceness," but by its repetition. Confirmation continues throughout the Christian life: daily renunciation of sin, the devil, and the world; daily renewal of faith; daily confession in word and deed of one's love for Christ. The rite of confirmation is one way of confessing Christ. There are many other ways, too, of confessing Christ.

Confirmation stands as a connecting link between baptism and the Lord's Supper. It is an affirmation of the validity of baptism in a Christian's daily life; it is an essential preparation for participation in the Lord's Supper. (In the case of one who is baptized as an adult, there is no real need of also having the act of confirmation as a special rite. It may well be made a part of the sacrament of baptism.) Confirmation prepares for Communion because it helps a person to examine himself before eating of that bread and drinking of that cup (I Cor. 11:28). Neither baptism nor confirmation is lastingly effective without continual participation in the grace of God.

THE LORD'S SUPPER

Jesus instituted the Supper for His disciples. It is apparent that it was meant to replace the Passover of the Old Testament, for it was instituted at the conclusion of the Passover meal. And we are told by St. Paul that Christ is our Passover (I Cor. 5:7). We may thus look for a resemblance between the two institutions. The Passover was celebrated in memory of the liberation from Egypt. It also had in it something of Messianic significance as we can sense from what John the Baptist said about Jesus: "Behold the Lamb of God who taketh away the sin of the world" (John 1:29).

In the memory of; unto remission of sin; until He comes. That is the meaning of the Supper. The Christian participates in obedience to Jesus. He confesses his faith in the Christ who came to redeem him. He appropriates by faith the fruit of Christ's redemption which is forgiveness. He confesses his faith in the Christ who is going to return (I Cor. 11:26).

The earthly elements in the Supper are bread and wine. Jesus did not say that they *changed* into something else (transubstantiation). He did not say that they *merged* with another element to form a new substance (consubstantiation). Nor did He say that the elements merely represented, symbolized, His body and blood. We are left to understand the words of Jesus in the light of what St. Paul tells us in I Cor. 10:16: "The cup of blessing which we bless, is it not the communion of the blood of Christ? The bread which we break, is it not the communion of the body of Christ?" That can mean only one thing: *the sacramental presence of Christ.* And what do we mean by a sacramental presence? A kind of presence uniquely attached to the Lord's Supper. There is a communion between the earthly and the heavenly elements. That makes the presence real and not merely symbolical.

We eat and drink the visible elements in a natural way. The body and blood are taken in a supernatural way. It is the glorified Christ who is present. That does not make Christ any less real. We know from the New Testament that Jesus assumed the use of His divine powers after the resurrection. He did not seem to be bound by what we call natural laws. But He was real. Even though He came through closed doors to visit His disciples, He ate food in their presence to prove that His presence was real.

As for the Reformed doctrine of Christ's localization in heaven, it seems that Biblical evidence rather favors Luther's teaching about the ubiquity (everywhereness) of Christ's (glorified) body. Note what Jesus said concerning Himself when He was here on earth: "And no man hath ascended up to heaven, but He that came down from heaven, even the Son of man which is in heaven" (John 3:13). That does not indicate any localization. And we are promised in Philippians 3:20-21 that our bodies shall be fashioned like His glorious body. So we cannot take the term "spiritual presence" of Jesus in the sacrament in the Calvinistic sense. For when Calvin said that Jesus is present spiritually in the Lord's Supper, he meant that the believer, in contemplating the suffering and death of Jesus, in faith elevates himself to the absent Christ, the Christ in heaven. By a sacramental presence we mean a real presence. That presence could be called spiritual if we eliminate the Calvinistic implications. For a spiritual presence can be both real and sacramental. One's belief concerning the Lord's Supper brings to a head all that one believes about the Bible and its proper interpretation. It shows what one believes about the incarnation, and the relationship of the human and divine natures in the person of Jesus. And because so many views come to a climax in the teaching about the Lord's Supper we find that it is precisely concerning this sacrament that denominational differences develop so readily

WHO SHOULD GO TO THE LORD'S SUPPER?

True disciples of Jesus: Those who live in a state of grace, who are concerned about their shortcomings, and who desire strength to live for the Lord; those who hate sin and who love the Lord and the Lord's people and the Lord's work; those who desire to grow in holiness.

WHY SHOULD I ATTEND THE LORD'S SUPPER?

1. Because Christ said: "This do in remembrance of me." My loyalty to Christ demands that I attend. He commands; I obey. As a Christian I have no business to single out the

commands of Christ that I wish to follow and then leave out the rest. One command is as serious as another.

2. Because I need the assurance of forgiveness which comes to me through the Supper. I need that individualized Gospel that the Supper gives me: "Given and shed for you [singular] unto the remission of sin!"

3. I need to confess my faith in Christ—faith in the Christ who came to save me; faith in the Christ who is going to return: "For as often as ye eat this bread, and drink this cup, ye do show [confess] the Lord's death until He comes" (I Cor. 11:26).

4. Remembering Christ, obeying Christ, confessing Christ strengthens my faith in Him.

5. I need the fellowship with other Christians: "For we being many are one bread, and one body; for we are all partakers of that one bread" (I Cor. 10:17).

6. I need the communion between myself and the Lord which I can experience in the Lord's Supper alone.

HOW THEN IS CHRIST PRESENT IN THE SUPPER OF THE LORD?

He is present sacramentally, i.e., a presence different from any other presence of the Lord because it is connected with the bread and the wine in the Lord's Supper. The Word of God makes this sacramental presence a real presence.

He is not present by transubstantiation, a *change* of the elements into body and blood; He is not present by consubstantiation, an adding of a new element to the bread and wine so as to *produce a third element;* He is not present merely *symbolically* so as to leave out a real sacramental presence.

The time of symbolism belongs to the Old Testament. The time of fulfillment and reality belongs to the New Testament. So declares St. Paul in Col. 2:16-17—as he enumerates Old Testament practices—"They were shadows of things to come; the body is of Christ." That means that the symbolism is completed in Christ.

Furthermore: The Lord's Supper is in the nature of a last

will and testament. That is not a place to use figurative language. Thus we conclude that the sacramental presence of Jesus is real; but that it is the glorified body of Jesus. Even in the state of the humiliation of Jesus (Phil. 2), He at times appeared in that glorified state.—He walked on the water; He was transfigured. We are not consuming material flesh and blood. But we partake of the glorified body and blood of Christ together with the bread and wine. The natural elements in communion are subject to mastication and digestion. The supernatural elements are not subject to such processes.

The following, somewhat imperfect diagram, may help to illustrate the three main views about the Lord's Supper:

Roman Catholic: Transubstantiation.

Bread, wine—body, blood.

Reformed view (non-Lutheran Protestants, varied). Symbolical presence.

Bread, wine—body, blood.

Evangelical Lutheran view: Sacramental presence.

Bread, wine—body, blood.

I Corinthians 10:16.

> *Christ was the Word and spake it;*
> *He took the bread and brake it;*
> *And what that Word doth make it,*
> *That I believe and take it.*
>
> [Engraved at the foot of the pulpit of the Church of Walton on Thames.]

Communicants are to partake of both the bread and the wine. It was so ordered by Christ.

WHO ARE WORTHY AND WHO ARE UNWORTHY COMMUNICANTS?

Worthy communicants are those who, upon self-examination, find themselves in need of grace because they want to continue to live in fellowship with Christ. They are His disciples. They may be weak; but their whole desire is to remain faithful to the Lord to the end. They repent of all personal faults and sins; they have a holy desire to be forgiven; they have a sincere resolve to shun all evil and to follow Christ.

Unworthy communicants are those who do not live in fellowship with Jesus, and who suppose that merely by complying outwardly with the custom of attending the Lord's Supper they can make up for all shortcomings and evils without any genuine change of heart.

Read I Corinthian chapters 10 and 11.

Lamb of God most holy!
Who on the cross didst suffer,
Patient still and lowly,
Thyself to scorn didst offer;
Our sins by Thee were taken,
Or hope had us for forsaken:
Have mercy on us, O Jesus!
[N. DECIUS]

We Believe in Church and State
(SECONDARY MEANS OF GRACE)

> *Take heed unto yourselves, and to all the flock, in which the Holy Spirit hath made you bishops, to feed the church of the Lord which he purchased with his own blood* (Acts 20: 28).
>
> *And Jesus said unto them: Render unto Caesar the things that are Caesar's, and unto God the things that are God's* (Mark 12:17).

THE CHURCH

The primary Means of Grace, as we have seen, are the Word of God and the sacraments. But the Lord has also provided agencies through which these means are administered, made available, and safeguarded.

The Church is of the utmost importance in preserving the Christian doctrines and the Christian way of life, and in bringing men into contact with the Word and the sacraments. The Church may be said to be the repository of the Means of Grace. The Church is divinely founded. It is made up of believers in Jesus Christ, people who have been called of God and who have obeyed His call. The Church is the society of consecrated people, "the communion of saints," as we have it in the Apostles' Creed.

In the Augsburg Confession the Church is defined as being "the congregation of saints, in which the Gospel is rightly taught and the sacraments rightly administered." It also says that true unity in the Church can be established by agreeing on the teachings of the Gospel and the administration of the sacraments. But it also admits that in the world where the Church exists, there will be hypocrites mingled with the true members. And also that even a minister might in some cases be a hypocrite; but the sacraments and the Word are not invalidated by such evil men. Recipients who truly believe in Christ receive what the Word declares.

The New Testament speaks about the Church as the bride of Christ, the body of Christ. The Church belongs to the Lord. (See Ephesians.)

The local congregation is the foundation of the whole Church organization. The Church began as a congregation, not as a hierarchy of bishops and priests, synods and dioceses. The Bible provides no one form for a valid church organization, or church government. That was left to the sanctified common sense of the Church itself, to be adjusted as the needs arose. But here we make good use of what the history of the Church has taught us.

Christians have always united in a Church. It is difficult to remain a Christian very long if one neglects the Church, the fellowship of believers. In Hebrews we read, "Do not neglect the assembling of yourselves together."

Christ is the head of the Church (Eph. 5:23; Col. 1:18). He has not resigned that headship to anybody, either on a temporary or permanent basis.

The Church exists for the following purposes: To unite and encourage God's people (II Tim. 3:16-17). To provide a place and a means for public worship. To keep Christians properly disciplined. To provide Christian fellowship (Acts 2:42; John 2:16). To propagate the Gospel (Matt. 28:19-20). To be the guardian of truth (I Tim. 3:14-15).

There are times in the New Testament when the church and the kingdom of God seem to mean the same thing. But ordinarily the church is a segment of the kingdom. The kingdom concept is larger than the church concept. As far as the visible, organized church is concerned, it is that portion of God's kingdom that lies within the period from the first Pentecost after the ascension of Jesus to His return to judge the living and the dead. The kingdom is larger. It includes the whole reign of God in both heaven and earth. If we think of the kingdom as the kingdom of grace, then we come closer to the true church of Christ which is made up of true believers.

St. Paul defines the kingdom of God as being "righteousness, peace and joy in the Holy Spirit" (Rom. 14:17). Jesus also stressed the purely spiritual side of the kingdom of God when He said: "The kingdom of God is within you" (Luke 17:20-21). To illustrate the meaning of the kingdom of God Jesus told many parables, and also taught the manner of entering into the kingdom. We may certainly say that a true follower of Jesus, a true member of His church, is also a member of God's kingdom. But we may not identify any one visible branch of the church with the kingdom of God as does the Roman Church.

THE MINISTRY

There is no room for a sacrificial priesthood in the New Testament Church. Ministers are not mediators, but witnesses. The pastoral office in the New Testament Church is a continuation of the prophetic office in the Old Testament and of the apostolate in the New Testament. It is not a continuation of the priesthood. Jesus was the last priest. In Him the priest and the sacrifice became one, and He sacrificed Himself once and for all (Heb. 9:28; 10:10, 12, 14, etc.).

The ministry is a divine office (I Cor. 12:28). It is not a distinct and separate order over and above other members in the Church. It need not be three-fold: bishop, priest, deacon. The congregational call is important (Acts 13:2-3). Ordination is a sacred dedicatory act by which a man is publicly inducted to the holy office of the ministry after he has been properly trained, examined, and called. The pastor of a church is to preach the Word, Law and Gospel, and administer the sacraments, visit the sick, encourage the saints, and invite the sinners to come to Christ and His church.*

THE HOME

The home is in some ways the most important institution on earth. Here lies the solemn duty of "teaching them to observe." The home was meant to be a vestibule of heaven, a

---

*For an excellent discussion of the ministry, read pages 181-186 in Mellenbruch: *The Doctrines of Christianity.*

church in miniature, the preserver of all that is good. The home is a divine institution, not an outgrowth of an evolutionary process (Gen. 2:18; Matt. 19:4-5).

To maintain the home, God provided for marriage between one man and one woman. Polygamy is not in the original divine order. Marriage is a divine institution. But it is also part of man's life in the state and in society. There can be no valid objection to civil marriage even though marriage by the ministry of the Church is to be preferred. And even a civil marriage should be blessed by the Church.

Christians should not be unequally yoked to unbelievers. A Christian ought to marry a Christian. The Roman Catholic decree called *Ne Temere,* laying down rules for mixed Roman and Protestant marriages, has no validity in the Bible. The decree is both un-American and un-evangelical.

Home, marriage, children, Christian instruction in the home —those are the foundations of a society that expects to endure.

The Bible knows of one, and at most, two, valid reasons for divorce: adultery and malicious desertion. The modern divorce mania stands condemned by the Bible, utterly condemned. (See Matt. 19:9 and I Cor. 7:15).

THE STATE

God ordained government (Rom. 13:1). Jesus said so (John 19:11). God has not decreed the kind of government under which men are to live. But He has decreed freedom. No one may enslave another under divine law. The state is to maintain order in society. It is to provide for man's well-being. It cannot prescribe rules for a man's conscience, but it can see to it that freedom to worship is maintained. The traditional Protestant teaching holds to the separation of Church and state. That means that the Church is not to dictate to the state nor the state to the Church. But since in many cases a citizen is both a member of the Church and a citizen of a state he must learn to live as a Christian citizen. Both Church and State are meant to serve God: the Church to provide for man's spiritual wants and the state to make it possible for a man to provide for his physical wants.

Christian citizens are to obey their governments. But God is to be obeyed rather than men. If the State commands things contrary to God's commandments the Christian should object. Christians may obey the state in regard to participation in just wars. The individual can hardly determine when a given war is just. However, one cannot invade the realm of the conscience of another even in such matters, and governments have recognized "conscientious objectors." It would take a strong personal conscientious conviction to go contrary to the will of a whole people. But conscience should be free.

Citizens owe obligations to their government. They are not to look for privileges only. Christian citizens should be very faithful in their every obligation to lawfully constituted governments. That does not mean that a Christian is to tolerate any kind of government. He is in duty bound to do all in his power to correct abuses, to improve conditions when selfish politicians fail to act. A Christian is not to forget that he is a citizen. And when moral issues are involved a Christian citizen should certainly let his light shine before men.

The Church as such should found no political party nor sponsor any given party. Through the ministry and its membership it should be outspoken for social justice and opportunity for all citizens to live a life commensurate with the dignity of a being created in God's image.

The State, according to our U. S. A. Constitution, has no right to favor any one church above another, nor to give financial support to any church for its religious program. The fundamental law of our land provides for the separation of Church and State. The State cannot pass laws hindering the Church in its public worship, and work of charity, unless a given cult or denomination becomes a public nuisance. We have in the United States of America freedom of worship.

The Church should demand no State support for its own religious program in any shape or manner whatsoever. If it is entitled to support it would soon obligate itself to control.

There should be no official recognition of the Roman Catholic Church by sending official or personal representatives to

Vatican City. If that is done to one church it should be done to all churches. But the Roman Church alone asks for such recognition.

Let the Church remain a Church. Let the State take care of its own functions—one of which is to see to it that citizens have the full freedom of worship.

Read Eph. 3; Romans 13.

Thou holy Church, God's city, shine,
High on His mountain founded!
Sing praise to Christ, thy king divine,
Who thee with walls surrounded;
Thy children He doth bless and sends
His peace to thee, thy strife He ends:
Now praise thy God, O Zion!

[M. B. LANDSTAD]

✿　✿　✿

God bless our native land!
Firm may she ever stand,
Through storm and night;
When the wild tempests rave,
Ruler of wind and wave,
Do Thou our country save
By Thy great might.

[C. T. BROOKS, J. S. DWIGHT]

We Believe in the Christian Way of Life

> *I therefore, the prisoner of the Lord, beseech you that ye walk worthy of the vocation wherewith ye are called* (Eph. 4:1).
> *Wherefore the rather, brethren, give diligence to make your calling and election sure: for if ye do these things, ye shall never fall* (II Peter 1:10).
> *Even so faith, if it hath not works, is dead, being alone* (James 2:17).
> (See Romans 2:17-24)

Christian experience comes out of the Christian faith. Today it is quite commonly stated that the Christian life is the sum total of Christian experience, and that faith is the result of such experience. That kind of view finally leads to the concept that one can have morality without religion. Preachers who hold such a view moralize a great deal, but say little or nothing about faith in Christ, repentance, and the work of the Holy Spirit. Of course, the Bible declares that faith without works is dead. But the Bible also declares that salvation by observing legal precepts is impossible. Thus we understand that the Biblical point of view is that a living faith in Christ issues in a Christian way of life. It is not a question of doctrine *or* life, but a matter of faith *and* life. A true Christian faith and a genuine Christian life must always go together. Morality without religion never worked very well. Religious faith without manifestation in moral living becomes dead formalism.

What are the distinguishing features of the Christian life? If we answer that question in Biblical language, we can say with St. Paul that it consists in putting off the old Adam (man's sinful inclinations), and putting on the new man (the ingrafted spiritual nature). That again is the same as using the two words *renunciation* and *faith*. Daily renunciation of sin, daily confession of faith in the triune God, daily renewal.

The Pauline epistles indicate very clearly what it is that we are to put off, to fight against. In Colossians he says we are to be "dead to wordly contacts." He warns against sexual immorality, filthy-mindedness, covetousness, lack of self-control, lying, slandering, telling smutty stories, etc. Then the apostle urges the Christian to put on the virtues of the Christian life: to be kind, humble, tolerant, ready to forgive others, ready to love others, and to live a life of thankfulness to the Lord. (See Ephesians and Galatians as well as Romans to learn what the results of faith should be.)

THE CHRISTIAN WAY OF LIFE IS A WAY OF PRAYER

Pray without ceasing (I Thess. 5:17).
And be ye thankful (Col. 3:15).

We have already mentioned prayer as an aid in sanctification. In other words, if one is to grow in his Christian life, he must pray. Prayer keeps a Christian in fellowship with God. Prayer is a God-given privilege. The Holy Spirit Himself is interested in our prayers; for it is He who teaches us to pray as we ought to pray. The effective prayer is Spirit-filled, childlike, utterly simple.

When we think of prayer, we nearly always think of asking for something. Yes, prayer is that; but it is more than that. It is speaking to God in our heart; to be attuned to our heavenly Father; to live in the atmosphere where Father and child meet, and to feel at home there; to be thankful to God continually. Prayer is at its best when "song and service blend," when work and prayer are so closely united that they can hardly be identified singly. "He prayeth best, who loveth best."

You learn to pray by praying. It sounds peculiar; but our

prayers sometimes become real only after we have prayed about our prayers. That means that we have to ask God for help to pray. And then our prayers somehow partake in the divine; for they come from the very depth of the human soul. "Out of the deep, I cry to Thee!"

Jesus taught His disciples to pray, and He gave them the perfect prayer, His prayer. Not that He ever prayed it with them. He could not do that. He never asked for the forgiveness of sin; for He did not have any. But He told His disciples to put that prayer on the same level as the prayer for daily bread. The fifth petition in the Lord's Prayer begins with "and." That connects it with the previous prayer for daily bread.

The Lord's Prayer bears a strong resemblance to the commandments. It puts God first: *Thy* name; *Thy* kingdom; *Thy* will. Then follow the other petitions concerning our own welfare and that of our neighbor's. Only when God gets His from us can we get ours from Him. There can be no real deliverance from evil until the name of God is honored, the kingdom of God established within the heart, the will of God made uppermost in our life.

God knows our needs. He included the prayer for daily bread for our body; for spiritual bread for our souls, which comes through forgiveness; for protection against falling when we are tempted to sin; for deliverance from all evil. It follows then that the kingdom, the honor, the glory belong to God. For prayer presupposes a God-centered life.

Our prayers are to be in the name of Jesus. "In my name," He said. Our prayers must be such that they can receive His approval, His sanction. And with His endorsement they are good in heaven. In His name we can ask for what seems both significant and insignificant. Do not worry about troubling God too much by your prayer. He loves to answer prayers. He does not become an errand boy when He answers our prayers. It only gives Him an opportunity to display His generosity. He loves that. He wants to be asked for things. He wants to be thanked.

Does God answer all prayers? Yes. But He answers many

prayers by saying *no*. And a "no" from a wise Father is a good answer.

THE CHRISTIAN WAY OF LIFE IS A LIFE OF WORSHIP

"Not forsaking the assembling of ourselves together, as the manner of some is; but exhorting one another: and so much the more as ye see the day approaching" (Heb. 10:25).

When we say that the Christian way of life is a way of worship, we mean worship of God in the public services on Sunday morning, and it means regular church attendance. But it also means private or personal devotion, worship of God in the home. Then it means a dedication to God of our whole life so that our daily work, too, becomes a worship-service.

In the New Testament we have a wonderful example of what a right worship-service is like. The story of the Pharisee and the publican in the temple tells it all (Luke 18:9 ff). It is important how we prepare ourselves for the service that we are to attend. The first part of the service takes place on the way to church. The second part is in the sanctuary itself. We read that two men went up into the temple to pray. But only one of them had a real meeting with God. That tells the difference in the results of their church attendance. In the presence of God the publican found himself a sinner; he begged for mercy and found it. The Pharisee compared himself with other people, and made out a good case for himself—self-satisfied, self-righteous; but not acceptable to God. Then comes the third part of the church service: the way home. That counts a great deal. That is when we begin to put into practice what we resolved to do when we met God. And the homeward way goes on into our environment, and into all the work for the kingdom of God.

In John 4 we learn that the thing that matters in our worship is not the *where* nor the *when*, but that our worship must be in spirit and in truth.

Outward ceremonies have their place. But we must be on our guard against formalism. Formalism can be a danger whether the service is liturgical or non-liturgical.

THE CHRISTIAN WAY OF LIFE IS A LIFE OF WITNESSING

"Ye shall be my witnesses," said Jesus. That makes every Christian a missionary. That is how the Gospel spread so rapidly in the early church. Go tell! That is the slogan of the church.

How shall I witness? Tell what Jesus has done for you. Invite the unchurched to come to church. Bring the children to Sunday school. Testify by your life in home and neighborhood. Show that the Christian life is *better* than the life in sin. Use whatever gift God gave you in His service. Anybody willing to work can find something to do for the Lord.

Again, it is well to remember that witnessing unto Jesus is not something we do at one time, when we have nothing else to do, or when we are dressed up in our best clothes. Witnessing is a constant process. If we cannot witness to Jesus when we are at our daily work, our witnessing at other times is likely to be quite ineffective. We witness by our living and by our giving.

Some people are called to full time service in God's kingdom here on earth. The call usually connects up with the talents that God gives us. If we are willing to be guided by God's Spirit we will find out God's will for our lives.

T IE CHRISTIAN WAY OF LIFE IS A LIFE OF STEWARDSHIP

1. *Stewardship of mind.*—In I Chron. 28:9 there is an admonition to King Solomon to serve God with a willing mind. God wants our mental powers to be dedicated to His service. God's Word provides an adequate remedy for mental depression, conflicts and tensions. "Thou wilt keep him in perfect peace, whose mind is stayed on Thee; because he trusteth in Thee" (Is. 26:3). When the mind is dedicated to God, the work of God progresses, because the people have a mind to work (Neh. 4:6). A mind dedicated to God is a humble mind, and accomplishes much as in the case of St. Paul (Acts 20:19; II Tim. 1:7).

2. *Stewardship of body.*—Says the apostle Paul: What? know ye not that your body is the temple of the Holy Ghost which is in you, which ye have of God, and ye are not your own? For ye are bought with a price; therefore glorify God in your body, and in your spirit, which are God's (I Cor. 6:19-20). Read also I Thess. 4:1-12, preferably in the translation by J. B. Phillips.

3. *Stewardship of time.*—It is well to remember with the Psalmist of old that my time is short (Ps. 89:47). Also with the wise man of old that there is a time and a season for everything (Eccl. 3:1-8). For us Christians, too, the admonition is that we are to redeem the time, because the days are evil (Eph. 5:16). And again with the Psalmist that our time is in the hand of the Lord (Ps. 31:15).

4. *Stewardship of talents.*—We are stewards of God's manifold gifts (I Peter 4:10). See Matt. 18:23 ff. Also Luke 12:41 ff; Matt. 25:14 ff.

5. *Stewardship of money.*—It is well to remember that all that we possess we have received from the Lord (I. Cor. 4:7), and that the gold and the silver belong to Him.—It is correct to say: "We give Thee but Thine own."

To become good stewards of our money we must do like the Macedonians, first give ourselves to the Lord (II Cor. 8:5). There should be no legalism about our giving. It is well to read II Cor., chapters 7, 8, 9, in regard to Christian giving. It is to be in proportion to a man's income (I Cor. 16:2). And the giving is to be both to God and to Caesar (government). Many advocate the giving of one-tenth of one's income to the work of the Lord. That is for each individual to decide.

THE CHRISTIAN WAY OF LIFE IS TO FIND EXPRESSION IN ALL HUMAN RELATIONSHIPS

The Pauline epistles are very clear in regard to the obligations one assumes, under the Gospel, to live a life of love. The apostle Paul begins with the *home.* Husband and wife are to live together in mutual love and respect. Children are to be obedient; but parents are not to provoke them by being needlessly severe. The problem between *servants and masters* is

also dealt with. Today we call it labor and management relationship. And how is it to be dealt with? Both parties are to
be mindful of their privileges and their obligations. The worker
is to give full time for full pay. And the manager is to treat
his worker as a fellow human being and to remember his own
accountability to God. (See in particular Col. 3:18, 4:1; Eph.
5:20, 6:9). The one word which describes all human relationships, according to the Christian view of life, is *mutuality*. This
again is based upon the fundamental concept that first and
foremost we all have certain obligations to God. What good
we have in life we have received from Him. To Him we are to
give an account. Out of a correct relation to God must develop
the correct relationships to our fellow men.

The Christian life is then to be dominated by the law of
love. And when a sinner has come to realize God's love, and
has accepted His gracious gift of salvation, he begins himself
to love. Love is the fulfillment of the law. Thus, God's saving
grace enables a sinner to do what he never could do by his own
efforts, namely, to live in harmony with the law of God. Saved
by grace he has power to begin living the life of love.

The Christian way of life is one of *prayer* and *devotion*, lived
in the atmosphere of the Holy Word, and sacramental grace.
It is also a way of *self-denial*. Many things that are not sinful
in themselves are given up by the true Christian if he feels
that his Christian life is not gaining by participation in them.
He is also guided by the principle that if a weaker person than
himself should be led into sin by doing what he, the Christian,
is doing—even if it is not sinful—he will not do it.

The Christian way of life is one of *joyful service*. There is
always something to do for others: teaching, visiting sick and
lonely people, work in the Church of various types. Not only
that: but the very vocation of the Christian becomes part of a
divine service. He feels that he is a partner with God in work-
ing out a great plan which has the glory of eternity in it. The
line between what men call spiritual and secular disappears
more and more, and for the Christian all of life belongs to
God. He does not do certain things for God and certain things

for himself. There is a beautiful harmony apparent in such a
life. The world is God's world. The Christian works for God.
That makes him a free man. True freedom comes from God
only.

THE CHRISTIAN WAY OF LIFE REACHES
FOR PERFECTION

The Christian is a sinner saved by grace. He lives in the
state of grace, not in the state of sin. But he is also aware of
his own human weaknesses and short-comings. As a matter
of fact just because he is a Christian he is now able to detect
sins he never saw before. Perfect holiness is not within his
grasp, for only God is perfectly holy. But, because the divine
nature dwells in the Christian, he strives for the very perfection to which he is called, and which he knows will be his
when he sees God face to face. (Read Phil., ch. 3).

He is growing up to maturity in Christ. He ceases to be a
child in his views; he becomes mature in Christ. And he follows the injunction of his Lord who told him to pray *daily*
for the forgiveness of sin. He says: Give us *this day* our daily
bread, *and* give us (this day) the forgiveness of our sins even
as we live in the spirit of forgiveness in our relationship to
others. He *believes* in the forgiveness of sin, and he thanks
God for it. *Forgiveness is the motivating power in the life of
a Christian.* And then the strange thing happens that the very
fact that he is a *forgiven* sinner makes him *hate* sin with all his
soul. Thus forgiveness comes to play the most important part
in the life of the Christian. *It is forgiveness that keeps him
from sinning.* "With thee is forgiveness that thou mayest be
feared" (Ps. 130:4). In the degree that he appreciates God's
merciful forgiveness he fights against all sin. And if he falls
in weakness he rises again in the strength of God.

The Christian life is a struggle. It was that to St. Paul and
all the other saints of God. (All true Christians are saints.)
Paul concluded his life by saying: "I have fought the good
fight of faith!" (Read II Tim., ch. 4.)

The *goal* of all Christian living and service is to glorify God.

That is the aim of the Christian life as it is lived here in the world, and it will be the content of the life lived in heaven.

The Christian way of life is concerned with the life which now is and the life to come: It is both this-worldly and other-worldly. The Christian lives and works in the world, but as Jesus said, he is not of the world. He does not identify himself with aims and purposes that never look beyond this present world. His final goal is the Father's house with the many rooms. The Christian way of life is one which seeks to make this a better world in which to live, which means to make it more of God's world. The Christian seeks to bring God to the world and the world to God. But he still needs heaven to crown it all. The Christian is a stranger and a pilgrim here. He "looks for a city which hath foundations, whose maker and builder is God."

Read Hebrews 11; Ephesians 4 and 5.

How fair the Church of Christ shall stand,
A beacon light in all the land,
When love and faith all hearts inspire,
And all unite in one desire
To be as brothers, and agree
To live in peace and unity.

'Tis all in vain that you profess
The doctrines of the Church, unless
You live according to your creed,
And show your faith by word and deed.
Observe the rule: To others do
As you would have them do to you.

O gracious God, wilt Thou my heart
So fashion in each secret part,
That Thou be sanctified in me,
Till Thee in heaven above I see,
Where holy, holy, holy Lord,
We sing to Thee with sweet accord.

[T. KINGO]

We Believe in the Second Coming
of Our Lord (Eschatology)

But the end of all things is at hand. Be ye therefore sober, and watch unto prayer (I Peter 4:7).

The same Bible that in the Old Testament foretells the first coming of Jesus declares that He is coming a second time. The first coming was for the salvation of the world; the second coming will be to judge the world according to the words spoken by the Savior, and the manner in which those words have been received.

The oldest creed of the whole Christian Church has a very brief statement about the second coming: "From whence he shall come to judge the quick and the dead." That is a brief affirmation, and no more. It gives no time, it enumerates nothing about circumstances, but it states plainly that the Church believes that the Lord is going to return.

It is rather peculiar that in the light of such a clear statement there should be people who deny completely the whole idea of the second coming of the Lord. It is equally peculiar that the Adventists and Jehovah's Witnesses (so-called) have attempted to tell us the date of the second coming (1853 and 1914).

Liberal theologians will hear nothing about the return of Jesus. They have reasons for such denial. Not believing in the deity of Jesus, how can they believe that He will return? And accepting the evolutionary view of the world, there is no room for anything as catastrophic as the end of the world. According to the evolutionary view of life, things just go on improving all the time. But the Christian view speaks about judgment, an accounting, an end. This fundamental belief, and this Biblical teaching, are now denied by many who still would like to call themselves Christian. Evangelical Christians hold that if you believe the Bible about the first coming of Jesus, you must believe the Biblical doctrine of His return to judge.

The doctrines about the last things are called eschatology. That involves a study about death, the intermediate state, the last times, the second coming of Christ, the resurrection, the final judgment, the end of the world, the eternal estate

DEATH

The Bible declares that death is the result of sin. It is spiritual as it separates man from God; it is temporal as it separates soul from body; it is eternal for those who die in sin without repentance and forgiveness, and, in that case, separates man from God forever. For redeemed sinners who die in the faith, spiritual death and eternal death are changed to spiritual and eternal life. Temporal death becomes an entrance into eternal life, and thus loses its terror.

THE INTERMEDIATE STATE

By the intermediate state we mean the time that elapses between the time of death of the individual and the final judgment. Thus the time of the intermediate state, as we count time, differs a great deal for each individual. Those who die in the Lord are in a state of bliss, not as complete as it will be when soul and body become united at the final resurrection. Those who die in an unrepentant state are in a state of misery, a misery which will be increased at the final judgment. (Read the story about the rich man and Lazarus in Luke 16.) The blessed will be in Paradise and the lost in Hades, in torment. No one passes from one place to the other. There is no teaching about a so-called purgatory in the Bible. The various passages used by the Roman Catholic Church to prove the existence of purgatory are not applicable (II Maccabees 12:39-46; Matthew 5:25, 12:32; I Cor. 3:11-15, 15:29; Rev. 21:27). When Paul is quoted in I Corinthians 3 as saying that they shall be saved, "yet so as by fire," he is not referring to any purgatorial saving, but to the seriousness with which a man ought to consider his soul's salvation here in time. "He personally will be safe, though rather like a man rescued from a fire," says the new translation by Rev. J. B. Phillips.

THE LAST TIMES

The Bible mentions several "signs of the times." The Gospel will be proclaimed to all nations. A remnant of Israel will be saved (see Romans). Antichrists and finally the antichrist will appear (see I John and Thessalonians). There will be wars and rumors of wars, a great falling away from the faith, and many other signs—such as lawlessness and religious indifference, the return of the Jews to Palestine (Isaiah 11:11-12; Daniel 12:7; Luke 21:24). But the time itself is not stated.

THE SECOND COMING OF JESUS

He will come to usher in the final judgment and the end of the world. The dead shall rise again: believers unto life eternal; unbelievers to eternal separation from God. Those who are alive when the Lord comes, and who believe, will be caught up into the clouds, we are told, to be with the Lord (I Cor. 15:51-52). Christ Himself said nothing about a millennium. It is therefore difficult to interpret Rev. 20:1-10. Lutherans have contented themselves by disowning any kind of chiliastic notion about Revelation 20—to identify the millennium with any earthly kingdom.

THE RESURRECTION

We believe in the resurrection of the body to be united with the departed soul. The body will be a glorified body, but real. There will be no limitations attached to the resurrection body

—no pain, no blemishes. (We speak about believers.) The unbelievers, too, will rise unto judgment. The resurrection occurs on the "last day," just before the final judgment.

THE FINAL JUDGMENT

All will appear before the throne of Christ. All will be judged by Him according to the words spoken by Him while He appeared among men as the one Redeemer. The righteous have nothing to fear. They have, in a sense, had their judgment already (see Romans 8). Men will be judged by the manner in which they have related themselves to the Gospel or to whatever light God saw fit to grant them. No man will be condemned unjustly.

THE END OF THE WORLD

The world, in its present form, will be destroyed after the judgment. But there will be a new heaven and a new earth, we are told. Then shall dwell righteousness in the earth (II Peter 3:12-13).

THE ETERNAL DESTINY

The unsaved will be in torment forever. The saved people will be in eternal bliss. To be separated from God is torment. To be separated from God forever is eternal death. To be with God forever is eternal life. To have eternal life one must believe in Jesus Christ. To reject Jesus is to reject life.

Read I and II Thessalonians.

> *Great God, what do I see and hear!*
> *The end of things created!*
> *The judge of mankind doth appear,*
> *On clouds of glory seated;*
> *The trumpet sounds; the graves restore*
> *The dead which they contained before;*
> *Prepare, my soul, to meet Him*

PART TWO

Supplementary Chapters

We Believe that the Lutheran Church Is Part of the Holy Christian Church

First, I thank my God through Jesus Christ for you all, that your faith is spoken of throughout the whole world (Rom. 1:8).

For I am determined not to know anything among you, save Jesus Christ, and him crucified (I Cor. 2:2).

The Holy Christian Church, which is the fellowship of true believers in Jesus Christ, was founded by Christ Himself. His redemptive work is the background, and the purpose of the church, is to perpetuate the fruits of His redemption until the end of time. The first members were the apostles, the immediate followers of Jesus. The Holy Spirit, promised by Jesus, came upon the apostles and established His abiding presence in the Church. This Church was intended to be catholic, i.e., universal. (In our Lutheran Churches we usually do not say that we believe in the holy Catholic Church, because Catholic has come to be associated with the *Roman* Catholic Church). Three thousand members came into the Church on its very birthday—Pentecost Sunday—the first Pentecost after the ascension of Jesus, approximately 30 A.D., in Jerusalem. They repented of their sins and were baptized. They were adults. But God made provision for the membership of children, too, as we have seen.

The Christian Church started as a *congregation*. The first congregation had the apostles themselves for leaders. They found more work than they could take care of, and so they told the congregation to select some assistants (deacons) to be consecrated by the apostles (Acts 6).

Soon other congregations were established in Samaria and in Syria and elsewhere. A certain connection seems to have been established between the original congregation in Jerusalem and the newly established congregations. Each new congregation had its leaders. In Philippians, ch. 1, Paul calls them *bishops* and *deacons* and the members are called *saints* (people consecrated to Jesus Christ). Now we know that the term bishop was used interchangeably with the term elder or presbyter. So there was an elder or a bishop or several elders in each congregation.

Two matters made it necessary for the churches (congregations) to form a larger organization. These were the matter of *discipline* in the congregations, and the matter of *heresy*, false teachings propagated by certain men in various parts of the church. Thus came into being a synod. And as the church grew, dioceses were formed. Some one had to preside at the synodical sessions. Some one had to head the diocese. So came into being the office of bishop—by about 150 A.D. distinguished from the local elder or pastor. The powers of the bishops increased greatly. They were looked upon as the successors to the apostles. And there was the Roman pattern of government to follow. The Romans had had their provincial governors, etc. The more extensive the Church became the more complex its government became. Some bishops were called metropolitans, others became known as patriarchs and archbishops. Five bishops were regarded as superior: those in Jerusalem, Antioch, Alexandria, Constantinople and Rome. The bishop in Rome finally claimed supremacy over all the bishops. This claim was supported strongly, in the 5th century, by the *Petrine theory*, a theory which claims that the apostle Peter was the chief of the apostles, that he had been given the power of the keys (Matt. 16:18-19), that he was the first bishop in Rome, and that to his successors, the Roman bishops, (pope, papa), were given the powers that Peter possessed. (Tertullian, a teacher in the early Church, claimed there could be no transfer of whatever powers Peter might have possessed). That made the Church a *Roman* Church. The popes wanted it to be Roman Catholic. (How can it be Roman and Catholic?)

The answer to the Petrine theory is simple. Peter was a leader; but his leadership in the Jerusalem congregation soon passed to James the Just, brother of the Lord (Acts 15). The Church was not built upon Peter, but upon Christ, and Peter's confession of faith in Him as the Son of God. (See I Peter). Peter had no powers over and above the other apostles (Matt. 18:18). It has never been *proved* that Peter was the first *bishop* in Rome. His so-called successors can claim no special powers inherited from Peter. The powers ascribed to Peter belonged to the whole Church. And even if it should be proved some day that St. Peter was bishop in Rome, that would not validate the claim of Roman pontiffs. Furthermore, the whole Church, in council assembled, in 451, decided that the bishops in Rome and Constantinople were to have equal powers. This the Roman bishop resented. And from the day of Gregory I, who became Roman bishop in 590 A.D., the Teutonic sections of Europe were converted to Christianity by Roman missionaries or people who yielded their allegiance to Rome. That strengthened Rome's claim. All of England did not accept Roman supremacy in the Church until 664 in the Synod of Whitby. St. Patrick and the early Irish Church were not Roman Catholic. But the Roman bishops (popes) gained western Europe. Eastern Europe did not accept Roman supremacy. The official schism between the two came in 1054: never fully united before; never since. So the Holy Christian Church of individual congregations became dominated by a strong episcopacy, headed by the Roman bishop, and we have a Western European Roman Catholic Church, and Orthodox Eastern Catholic Churches. The *government* of the Church tended to be centralized in Rome and Constantinople.

In *doctrine* the early Christian Church held fast to the

apostolic teachings. It stressed the fact that Jesus of Nazareth was the promised Messiah, who had lived, taught, worked miracles, had died on the cross and had risen from the dead on Easter Sunday. A call went out to men everywhere to repent and believe in Jesus and be baptized unto the remission of sin.

Letters written by St. Paul and some of the other apostles explained more fully the meaning of the life, death and resurrection of Jesus. Then also came into being the written Gospels supplanting the oral Gospel. Here was told the story about Jesus. Men heard the Gospel. Some believed and were saved. Congregations were established. The faith was propagated. Every Christian was, in a sense, a missionary. The Gospel message spread rapidly. But the Gospel message was always in danger of being perverted. Men did not like to be told that they must be saved by grace alone. They wanted to contribute something themselves. Then there was the danger of Judaism and its interpretation of Christianity, a problem St. Paul deals with in Galatians. Heathen philosophers adapted part of Christianity to their own views. Some attempted to bring about a compromise between Christianity and various non-Christian religions and philosophies.

When Gregory I sent out missionaries to the heathen, he instructed them to compromise, to wean the heathen gradually from their heathen ways to Christianity. That resulted in many heathen practices sneaking into the Church. Then as the Roman bishops became more and more powerful many new doctrines were added.

The early Church knew only two sacraments. The Roman Church in the later Middle Ages (as well as now) had seven. Purgatory was introduced officially by Gregory I. Transubstantiation was made the official doctrine about the Lord's Supper in 1215. The way of salvation by grace alone became one largely made up of human merits obtained by certain good works performed. The Church fathers and tradition came to stand on an equality with the Bible. There was a grave danger that the words of men would replace the Word of God.

In the history of public *worship* the story is the same as in government and doctrine: from the simple to the complex. The earliest public worship was patterned after the worship service in the Jewish Synagogue. There were some songs and prayers, reading of the Scriptures and sermons, explaining the Word of God, and admonishing believers to live a truly Christian life. Baptism and the Lord's Supper were administered.

As time went on permanent meeting places were established, churches were built, and the services tended to become more formal. The tendency in religion seems to be towards formalism. The pastor became supplanted by the priest, the intermediary. The Lord's Supper came to be looked upon as a sacrifice to God instead of a memorial of the great sacrifice made once for all by Christ. And so the priest is there to offer up that sacrifice.

During the Middle Ages the idea of pilgrimages developed. Adoration of saints came into prominence. The Virgin Mary came to hold an ever increasingly important place both in worship and life. There are beginnings of that tendency in the 4th Century. But in the Roman Catholic Church Mary has become more and more important until today she has been called the "only gate to heaven, and none shall enter except through her." The Roman Church tended to forget Him who said: "Come unto me all ye who labor and are heavy laden and I will give you rest." The Pauline doctrine of justification by faith alone without the deeds of the law (Rom. 3) was covered up by man-made decrees and doctrines

The Christian *life* in the early Church had been a simple expression of love in all walks of life. The Gospel of equality before God had been preached everywhere. Men could be Christians in all walks of life and no one profession was regarded as essentially any more holy than another. Obedience and honesty characterized Christians. Purity of life was noted as a result of the acceptance of the Gospel. Marriage was held in high esteem. Clergy as well as lay people entered into marriage. St. Peter himself had been a married man. St. Paul found it convenient to remain single.

Then came the *Romanized* Church with its decrees of celibacy, and its emphasis upon the importance of the monastic life. Here one can again discern the influence of heathen philosophies of life. (There were monks and nuns both in Hinduism and Buddhism before the birth of Christianity.) The monastic life became the highest ideal. Secular pursuits were necessary, but not particularly blessed. The whole Christian life became less spontaneous than in the early Church, and became entangled in a lot of outward observances.

Of course, there was a Holy Christian Church during both the ancient period of history as well as during the Middle Ages. Such a Church was made up of true believers in Jesus. And such believers were found inside of the visible Church. But it was difficult to learn the Biblical way of salvation in a Church where so many non-Biblical doctrines had gained a foothold.

Voices of *reformers* were heard down the centuries. Long before Luther appeared on the scene there were men like Peter Waldo in France, Wycliff in England, Savonarola in Italy, Huss in Bohemia who called for a return to the simple Gospel, a return to the simple teachings of Apostolic Christianity, a return to faith in the human-divine Savior as man's only redeemer, a return to St. Paul's teaching about the forgiveness of sin through faith in Christ (justification by faith). Also there was a strong demand for the dissemination of the Word of God among the people in their own language. In France it was Lefevre d' Etaples who made a clear statement of such demands, and he, too, did it before Luther, and contemporary with Luther.

On the question of final authority in the Church, it is interesting to note that long before Luther's time, there had been a demand to reinstate the general Church council as authority above the pope. It came about in this way: the papacy sunk to such low levels, and interfered so generally in the affairs of government all over Europe, that the French government exiled Pope Boniface VIII and set up the next pope, and his successors, in Avignon, France, 1309-1378. That period in

Church history is called the Babylonian Captivity of the Papacy. That was followed by the Great (Western) Schism, 1378-1417. To heal the schism Gregory XI returned to Rome in 1377. But some cardinals in Avignon elected their own pope. The Church now had two heads. Then a Church council was summoned and deposed both popes, and elected a new one. As the two who were deposed refused to be deposed there were now three popes. The Council of Constance, 1414-1418 healed the schism in the Church; but it left the impression that the general council of the Church was above the pope. That impression has been wiped out by the Roman pontiffs as can be seen from the declaration of papal infallibility in 1870 by Pope Pius IX. Thus we see that the Roman Church had lots of trouble before the Reformation in the 16th century.

Under the domination of the papacy the Church became *Romanized*—the whole Church had to be ruled from Rome. Religion became *externalized*—religion was made too dependent upon outward observances, became less personal. The Roman Church became secularized, became part of the world in which it existed, became a worldly empire. The popes became secular rulers like kings and emperors, and claimed overlordship over all kings and emperors. The Roman Church had come to deviate from the Apostolic Church in *government* and *doctrine, worship* and *life*.

LET US NOW LOOK AT THE REFORMATION

The Reformation is not a break in the history of the Church. It is an *affirmation* of faith in the apostolic Church and in the Scriptural record. The Reformation is a *charge* against the Roman Catholic Church that in becoming Roman it had ceased to be Catholic, and had in reality departed from the real apostolic faith in many vital points. The Reformation is an attempt to get the whole Church back on the main track, on which it had started out, and to continue it on that track as a body of believers in Jesus, witnessing unto Jesus, the Christ of God, and the only true and infallible head of the Christian Church.

Martin Luther (1483-1546) became a reformer in the Church simply because he asked how a sinner could discover a gracious God. The Roman Church gave him no satisfactory answer. He found the answer to his question in the Bible as he found the Christ of the Bible. Luther's own religious experience determined his course in the Reformation. He found the central theme of the whole Bible to be justification by faith. That principle determined his whole outlook upon life.

John Calvin (1509-1564), the French reformer, began with the idea of the sovereignty of God, and predestination. He learned much from Luther, but his approach was quite different. But, he, like Luther, wanted a church that was in complete harmony with the Bible.

There were other reformers such as *Zwingli* in Switzerland; *John Knox* in Scotland; *Cranmer* in England. Luther was ably assisted by *Philip Melanchthon,* and others. Space here forbids us to enter into details. Suffice it to say that out of the Protestant Reformation in general, and the Lutheran Reformation in particular, came three great religious principles:

1. *The Material Principle* which teaches that justification is by faith. Forgiveness of sin is obtained by God's grace, accepted in faith by a repentant sinner.

2. *The Formal Principle* which teaches that the Bible is the final authority in the matter of Christian faith and conduct. Popes and church councils might err. The Bible, taken in its entirety, reveals the full truth.

3. *The Social and Ecclesiastical Principle* which teaches that all believers are priests before God; they may read and interpret the Bible. The pastor in the Church does not belong to a special *order;* he holds a sacred office in the Church. He is not a mediating priest between the people and God, but a minister of the Gospel, witnessing unto Jesus, administering the sacraments, caring particularly for the spiritual needs of the people. All Christians have direct access to God through Christ, the only mediator between God and man.—And as for the interpretation of the Scriptures, the third principle of the Reformation does not guarantee that all readers of the Bible

can understand everything in the Bible. But the teaching about sin and grace, a teaching upon which all other Biblical teachings depend, can be understood. The way of salvation is clear. —When St. Peter says in II Peter 1:20-21 that no Scripture is of private interpretation, he refers to the *writing* of the Bible, not the *reading* of it.

The reformers agreed on two sacraments even while they differed somewhat on their interpretation.

Luther produced his *Small Catechism* in 1529 as a brief summary of the fundamentals of the Christian religion. The same year he also published his *Large Catechism.* In 1530 came the *Augsburg Confession,* and in 1531 the *Apology* (defense) of the Confession. In 1537 Luther wrote a summary of his faith in the *Schmalcaldic Articles.* Then in 1577 Lutheran scholars produced the Formula of Concord. All these six special Lutheran Confessions make up what is called the *Book of Concord. The Lutheran Church was and is a Confessional Church.* Says the Augsburg Confession: "Our churches with common consent do teach," etc.

From Germany evangelical Lutheranism spread to Sweden (1527), to Denmark and Norway in 1536-37, and from Sweden to Finland. The Baltic provinces were strongly influenced by Lutheranism. Iceland also became Lutheranized. And since that early day in the 16th Century there are now Lutherans in all lands, "from Greenland's icy mountains to India's coral strand."

The Lutheran Church is the mother church of the Reformation, of Protestantism. It came into being because evangelical Christians wanted freedom in conscience so they would not have to forsake the Gospel. The Roman Catholic authorities would not grant it. *Thus they, the Roman authorities, disrupted the Church.* The Lutheran Church claims to be a part of the Church universal, founded by Jesus Christ. It never left the Scriptures and the Church catholic. It is the largest Protestant denomination in the world. It is Protestant because it protests against the abuses that led the Roman Church away from the central idea in the Church as established by Jesus. But it is

Protestant far more significantly because it stands for the full Gospel, for salvation by grace, for the whole counsel of God, for the whole Bible, pure, undivided, undefiled. Whatever is Biblical must be Lutheran. Anything in the Lutheran Church proved by the Bible to be unbiblical would have to go!

LUTHERANS IN THE U. S. A.

Lutherans left Europe for America at rather early dates. Some left because they sought more religious freedom, but most of them left their respective homelands to find better economic opportunities for themselves in the land which had been discovered at the very time that the Reformation began in the Church.

The Lutherans have been in the United States of America since colonial days. An expedition of Scandinavian Lutherans, under Captain Jens Munk, a Dane, came to the Hudson Bay in 1619. The chaplain was Pastor Rasmus Jensen. He preached a Christmas sermon there in 1619. The Canadian government has seen fit to honor the expedition by erecting a monument in honor of the expedition. It has been stated that the French explorers learned something from this expedition.

Dutch Lutherans, and some Scandinavians, came to New Amsterdam as early as 1624.

Then the Swedish Lutheran colony at Delaware in 1638 became a milepost in American history.

A great wave of German immigrants came to Pennsylvania beginning in about 1683. The story of their great patriarch, Henry Melchior Muhlenberg, 18th century, is an outstanding chapter in American Lutheranism and in American history.

In the second quarter of the 19th century, and throughout that century, Lutherans came from Norway, Sweden, Denmark, Iceland, Finland and other European nations. A group of German Lutherans settled in Perry County, Missouri, and became the founders of the Missouri Synod.

We cannot here enter into detail concerning the history of

the Lutheran Church in America. Suffice it to say that from the outset Lutherans felt at home in this land of free people, and they have been found on the side of liberty from 1776 to the fight for the union in 1861 and on. Pennsylvania German Lutherans were prominent in George Washington's army. Norwegian Lutherans in Wisconsin and other states rallied to the cause of the Union. Lutherans in the border-states helped swing the election in favor of Lincoln. Frederick Muhlenberg, a son of the great Lutheran, Henry Muhlenberg, was the first speaker of the House of Representatives.—Lutherans have been identified with American life from the very beginning. It is no more a foreign Church than the others.

LUTHERAN SYNODS AND FEDERATIONS

Naming the many nations from which the Lutherans came to America gives an indication of the reasons for the kind of organizations they formed in this land of their adoption. Their first organizations were congregations. And when congregations united to form synods they were organized pretty much along the lines of the national origins of the adherents. However, no matter where they came from, these Lutherans adhered to the Sacred Scriptures, Luther's Small Catechism, the Augsburg Confession. So they were not as different one from the other as it looked by the many Synodical organizations.

The earliest synodical organization was the Pennsylvania Ministerium, 1748. The first attempt at synodical organization among Scandinavian Lutherans was in 1846. Numerous synods were organized. And then a merging process began.

In 1890 there was a merger of three Norwegian synods into one to form the United Norwegian Evangelical Lutheran Church of America. The Norwegian Augustana Synod of 1870; the Conference (Norwegian-Danish) of 1870; the anti-Missourian Brotherhood of 1887 constituted the union of 1890.

In 1917 there was again a merger of Norwegian-American synods: The United Norwegian of 1890; the Norwegian Synod of 1853, and the Hauge Synod of 1876 (originally of 1846) joined to form the Norwegian Lutheran Church of America.

The name was changed in 1946 to The Evangelical Lutheran Church.

In 1918 there was a merger of The General Council of 1866; The General Synod of 1820, and the United Synod of the South of 1863 to form the *United Lutheran Church of America.*

In 1930 the joint Synod of Ohio of 1818; the Iowa Synod of 1845; the Buffalo Synod of 1845, and the First Evangelical Synod in Texas merged to form the *American Lutheran Church.*

In 1872 the Synodical Conference was organized, made up of the Missouri Synod of 1847 and the Wisconsin Synod of 1892.

The American Lutheran Conference was organized in 1930, made up of five synods, but it has now ceased to exist.

In 1960 The American Lutheran Church was organized by the merging of the American Lutheran Church of 1930; the United Evangelical Lutheran Church of 1878, and the Evangelical Lutheran Church of 1917. In 1962 the Lutheran Free Church of 1897 became a part of this church body.

The Lutheran Church in America was organized in 1962. Merging to form this body were the American Evangelical Lutheran Church of 1884; the Augustana Evangelical Lutheran Church of 1860; The Finnish Evangelical Lutheran Church in America of 1890, and the United Lutheran Church in America of 1918.

In 1918 the National Lutheran Council was organized. And in 1923 The Lutheran World Conference came into being. It was changed to the Lutheran World Federation in 1947.

In the U.S.A., Lutherans form the third largest Protestant denomination. Most Lutherans in America now belong to one of the three larger bodies: The American Lutheran Church of 1960, The Lutheran Church in America of 1962, or the Lutheran Church—Missouri Synod of 1847.

The National Lutheran Council has proved a most excellent organization for the participating synods in doing all the work of an inter-synodical nature. Lutheran World Action is doing a great work in relieving misery and want everywhere, rebuilding torn down churches, bringing new hope to many lives, maintaining orphaned missions, etc.

And what does the Lutheran Church stand for? "A change-less Christ for a changing world."

LUTHERANS AND THE CHURCH YEAR

Remember the Lord Jesus Christ (II Tim. 2:8).

The idea of the "church year" was no doubt derived from Jewish practices. It dates back to the early church which began to celebrate Easter in memory of the resurrection of Jesus. Then came Pentecost, in memory of the founding of the Church, and in the 4th century the observance of Christmas, in memory of the birth of the Savior of the world. When fully developed we see the whole plan of redemption set before us, particularly as that plan centers in Jesus.

Christmas is the festival of the Father who gives His Son; Easter the festival of the Son who takes back His own life from death; Pentecost the festival of the Holy Spirit, who comes to abide in the church through Word and Sacraments.

New Year's Day of the church year is the first Sunday in Advent, four Sundays before Christmas—a period of expectation and preparation. Then comes Christmas and the secular New Year. In the church year Epiphany follows New Year. Epiphany means to make known and celebrates the coming of the wise men and the manifestation of Jesus to them. This is a period in which the missionary enterprise of the Church is emphasized. Then comes Lent in preparation for Easter. Lent is a period of self-denial and meditation upon the suffering of Jesus. The proper observance of Lent is "to starve thy sin, and not thy bin, and that's to keep thy Lent." The last week before Easter is called Passion Week or Holy Week in which we have Holy Thursday or Maundy Thursday in memory of the institution of the Lord's Supper, and Good Friday in memory of the death of Jesus. Easter commemorates the fact of the bodily resurrection of Jesus. Pentecost, 50 days after Easter, commemorates the outpouring of the Holy Spirit upon the apostles of Jesus and the founding of the Holy Christian Church. Then comes Trinity Sunday reminding us of our faith in a triune God, inseparably connected with Christianity as a redemptive religion. The Sundays after Trinity Sunday are dedicated to the presentation of the whole program of the Church. The work in self-discipline, the work for others, the ushering in of the reign of God on earth by making men everywhere the followers of Jesus Christ.

LUTHERANS AND LITURGY

Let all things be done decently and in order (I Cor. 14:40).

That thou mayest know how thou oughtest to behave thyself in the house of God, which is the church of the living God, the pillar and ground of the truth (I Tim. 3:15).

The Lutheran reformation was a conservative reformation. Luther himself believed that whatever was not contrary to the Scriptures might well be retained in the reformed congregations. Zwingli, on the other hand, worked on the principle that only what was directly commanded in the Bible should be allowed in the churches. It seems that four hundred years of church history have justified Luther in his stand. At any rate we note a tendency to moderate liturgical services in many churches that have Zwinglian and Calvinistic backgrounds.

The Lutheran Church in America works on the principle that the congregations decide such matters as order of service, etc. But again, the value of unity and uniformity is observed.

There is a warning in the Augsburg Confession, Article 28, that should not be forgotten: *"There are monstrous disputations concerning the changing of the law, the ceremonies of the new law, the changing of the Sabbath Day, which all have sprung from the false belief that there must needs be in the Church a service like the Levitical, and that Christ had given commission to the apostles and bishops to devise new ceremonies as necessary to salvation. These errors crept into the Church when the righteousness of faith was not clearly enough taught."*

The Lutheran Church uses a liturgical service in harmony with the early Christian Church. The proclamation of the Gospel is the center of the service. Everything else in the service contributes to that central act of worship: to give God an opportunity to reach the soul.

There can be a Lutheran Church without the use of vestments, candles and various ceremonies. And the church can be evangelical. But again, we note the pattern of the early Church, and the many variations in the churches without liturgy, and we retain our liturgical services. And we can still be evangelical—perhaps even more so. We are made aware of the church more than of the individual pastor. The church is the church of Christ, not of an individual minister. We are made aware of the fact that our own congregation belongs to a large household of the faith, a communion of saints. We sense something of the unity of the church.

Liturgy is valuable as long as it serves its intended use and purpose. In all churches whether liturgical or not, it is well to be on guard against formalism and externalism in religion. "God is a Spirit: and they that worship him must worship him in spirit and in truth" (John 4:24).

If any church has less than Jesus Christ and Him crucified, and risen from the dead, Jesus the incarnate Son of God—it has too little. If any church has more than Jesus Christ, and His completed salvation, it has too much.

THE LUTHERAN CHURCH AND CHURCH GOVERNMENT

The Lutheran Church does not believe that there is any one divine form of church government. Government is pretty much a matter of expediency. But various historical patterns offer a solution.

Maintaining the sovereignty of the congregations, the Lutheran Church nevertheless organizes its congregations into districts and synods to facilitate the work of the Church. The synod has delegated powers. A president of a given synod is elected by the synodical convention. In European Lutheran Churches the episcopal system is commonly used. There, too, in many instances, the churches are state churches. In the

U.S.A. Lutherans use a combination of congregationalism, presbyterianism and the episcopal system.

Read Acts 1-8

THE LUTHERAN CHURCH AND ITS WORK

The work of the Lutheran Church is to glorify Jesus Christ, and to make Him increasingly available to all men everywhere. To help sinners find God so they can be reconciled to Him. That is the real mission of the whole Christian Church. For it is the teaching of God's Word that men ought to seek God's kingdom first, and the other things will then be added. It is therefore the primary task of the Church to preach the Word of God, the law which demands, and the Gospel which gives.

Instruction in God's Word is absolutely essential, from infancy and all the way up to and including college level and beyond. *Teach them to observe!* To make Christ known the Church has an educational program; it must instruct people in the Word of God. It must train ministers and missionaries. The educational program of the Church is part of her mission program.

Then the Church must send out missionaries to heathen lands. "Go tell!" said Jesus. "Make disciples of all nations!" A Church that fails in her foreign missions fails in everything else.

"Begin in Jerusalem!" Begin at home. Preach the Gospel. Win the unchurched. Win the back-sliders. Organize congregations. Call pastors. Assistance for such work must come from the synodical treasury until newly formed congregations can take care of themselves.

Be ye merciful! Visit the sick! "Whatsoever ye have done unto one of these little ones, ye have done it unto me!" Work of charity. Yes, that is the work of the Church. For "the soul of charity is charity for the soul." Help the lonely ones, the homeless ones, the old people, little children, those who have strayed from the narrow path. What a tremendous work!

A great program: *Education. Home Missions and Church*

Extension. Foreign Missions, evangelizing the heathens. Work of mercy: Homes for children and the aged; rescue homes; home finding and welfare work of all kinds. Missions to seamen. Pensions for old ministers and their wives or widows.

A great deal to do, and the privilege of each church member to participate in such an extensive kingdom program.

Then there is what is perhaps the most important work, the maintenance and up-keep of the local congregation, its buildings and organizations. There are salaries, for the laborer is worthy of his hire. Work among the young people: Luther Leagues, Bible camps, choirs. All to win and hold young and old people for Christ. And lay people are needed. The whole community ought to be evangelized. The ministers cannot reach all that should be reached. You are called to be a laborer in the vineyard of the Lord, and you are called upon to use whatever talents the Lord gave you.

WHY BELONG TO THE CHURCH?

1. I need the Church and the Church needs me.

2. To honor my Savior. The Church is His. He bought it with a price. He is the head. To be united to Him one must be united with the Church, His body.

3. Alone one easily becomes lukewarm and cold. Many together accomplish more for God and fellowmen.

4. The Church has the Means of Grace in her midst. Unsaved sinners need to hear the Word; saved sinners need both Word and sacraments. No other institution has been delegated to proclaim the Gospel of grace and to administer the sacraments.

5. If I want the blessings from the Church I ought to share in the burdens.

6. Rightly understood there is no salvation outside of the Church. That is the normal and ordinary way. There are exceptional cases where church membership, in a visible church organization, could not be acquired.

7. As a saint I ought to belong to the communion of saints.

8. I ought to belong to the Church, because it is the greatest agency in any community for upholding high moral standards. It is the most worthwhile community center. If I believe in social and economic justice I ought to help the Church in proclaiming the principles that lead to such justice: to get right with God first that I might get right with fellow-humans!

A mighty fortress is our God,
A trusty shield and weapon;
Our help is He in all our need,
Our stay, whate'er doth happen;
For still our ancient foe
Doth seek to work us woe:
Strong mail of craft and power
He weareth in this hour;
On earth is not his equal.

Stood we alone in our own might,
Our striving would be losing;
For us the one true man doth fight,
The man of God's own choosing.
Who is this chosen One?
'Tis Jesus Christ, the Son
The Lord of hosts, 'tis He
Who wins the victory
In every field of battle.

And were the world with devils filled,
All watching to devour us,
Our souls to fear we need not yield,
They cannot overpower us;
Their dreaded prince no more
Can harm us as of yore;
His rage we can endure;
For lo! his doom is sure,
A word shall overthrow him.

Still must they leave God's Word its might
For which no thanks they merit;
Still is He with us in the fight,
With His good gifts and Spirit.
And should they, in the strife
Take kindred, goods, and life,
We freely let them go,
They profit not the foe;
With us remains the kingdom.

[M. LUTHER]

Wherein Evangelical Lutherans Agree
or Disagree with Other Christians

*One Lord, one faith, one baptism, One God
and Father of all, who is above all, and
through all and in you all* (Eph. 4:5-6).
Prove all things; hold fast that which is good
(I Thess. 5:21).
*Beloved, believe not every spirit, but try the
spirits whether they are of God: because many
false prophets are gone out into the world*
(I John 4:1).

AGREEMENTS

Lutherans have much in common with other evangelical
Christians. In the confessions of many non-Lutheran churches
there is an acceptance of the canonical books of the Old Testament and the New Testament as the Word of God. Evangelical Lutherans agree.

The Lutheran Church accepts the three* ecumenical (general) creeds as being correct statements of the Christian faith,
in harmony with the Scriptures. It therefore agrees with all
denominations on that point if expressed in their confessions.

Lutherans and other evangelical Christians accept two sacraments or ordinances: Baptism and the Lord's Supper. (Some
sects and cults ignore the sacraments.)

Lutherans, and nearly all evangelical churches, accept the
ministry in the Church as an office rather than an order. Angli-

---

*The Apostolic, the Nicean, the Athanasian.

cans and Episcopalians are agreed in accepting the ministry as a threefold order: bishop, priest, deacon.

Lutheran Christians are Trinitarians. So are all orthodox, evangelical Christians.

Evangelical Christians are agreed upon the view that Christianity is a personal matter. A decision must be made. All agree upon teaching that conversion is necessary, if a person who does not live in fellowship with God, expects to be saved.

Evangelical Christians agree concerning the teaching that salvation is by grace, though legalism creeps in, at times, in some denominations.

Evangelical Christians agree on a future state in which there will be rewards and punishments meted out. An individual will be judged on the basis of his relationship to Jesus and the Word will judge him. Evangelical Christians believe in the second coming of Christ.

Evangelical Christians believe in the supernatural, in miracles, in the virgin birth of Jesus.

Evangelical Christians agree on the teaching about man's fall into sin, on the guilt of sin, and on original sin. They also, therefore, agree on the necessity of the atonement by Jesus Christ, the Son of God, who died in our stead. They accept the substitutionary character of the atonement. They believe in the incarnation of Jesus—that the word became flesh and dwelt among us. And they believe in the resurrection of Jesus and in our own resurrection on the last day.

There is a fairly general agreement that the chief work of the Church is to preach the Gospel, to work both at home and abroad for the extension of God's kingdom, to maintain educational institutions, etc.

The liberal wings of the non-Lutheran churches, however, have come to accept the social gospel—ushering in of the kingdom of God here and now by means of human effort.

In their relationship to Roman Catholicism evangelical Protestants unite in repudiating the papacy, and the five sacraments over and above baptism and the Lord's Supper.

Evangelical Protestants hold certain Roman Catholic teachings to be un-Biblical, such as: purgatory, adoration of Mary and the saints, transubstantiation, the sacrifice of the mass, the equality of tradition with the Bible, and that salvation is merited, in part, by good deeds.

Protestants object to the enforced celibacy of the clergy and to the monastic life as being in any way more meritorious than the ordinary Christian life.

Protestants object to the autocracy in the Roman Church: it is dominated by the clergy. Protestants object to the Roman Catholic mixing of church and state, and the world politics of the Vatican. Protestantism objects to the externalism and the formalism in the Roman Church. The chief objection is to the additions made to the completed atonement of Jesus, the adding of mediators to the One who is declared in the Bible to be the one and only mediator between God and man, Jesus the Christ (John 14:6; I Tim. 2:5). They, therefore, strenuously object to making Mary the gate to heaven, and that none can enter except through her.

DISAGREEMENTS AMONG PROTESTANTS

From what we have said above it would appear that there could be no disagreements among the Protestant denominations. But the sad fact remains that there are disagreements.

Why are there disagreements? (1) Differences in interpretation of the Bible. The Reformed Churches rationalize where Lutherans take the Bible at face value. (2) Sin has a part in all our differences. (3) We see in a glass darkly, as St. Paul says. In this sinful world we lack a perfect vision. (4) Personal reasons: self-aggrandizement. Men fail to walk humbly before God. Set themselves above church and Bible and then set up their own little "church." Some want to spite other churches. Pecuniary gains. (5) Failure to let the Bible interpret the Bible. (6) Misunderstanding of what is meant by grace alone. (7) Sects thrive on neglected truth; i.e., the historic churches may have under-emphasized certain beliefs and practices, such as prayer for the healing of the sick. (8) Too much emphasis on one teaching and failing to remember the whole counsel of God. (9) Lack of historical sense. Failure to see God's hand in the history of the Church. (10) Zeal without knowledge (Rom. 10:2).

Then it must be remembered that nearly all Reformed Churches are split wide open by modernism or liberalism. Many Presbyterians, Methodists, Baptists, Congregationalists and Episcopalians repudiate evangelical Christian beliefs. They deny the deity of Jesus, the unique, divine inspiration of the Bible, the vicarious atonement, the guilt of sin, salvation by faith, the second coming of the Lord. When such a situation develops then there is bound to be differences both between evangelical Lutherans and the Reformed Churches as well as within the Reformed family of churches.

WHEREIN DO LUTHERANS AND REFORMED CHRISTIANS DIFFER THE MOST

1. On the interpretation of the Bible. The tendency in Reformed circles is to rationalize the Word of God. They, like the Roman Catholics, accuse the Lutherans of oversimplification, when Lutherans find justification by faith the key to the whole Bible.

2. On the interpretation of the sacraments. To most of the Reformed Churches the sacraments are mere symbols. They do not believe in sacramental grace. Baptism is defined as an "outward sign of an inward change." The Lord's Supper is essentially a memorial service. We have seen the Lutheran interpretation of the sacraments and sacramental grace, in previous chapters.

There are so many differences within the reformed family of churches that one would have to describe each denomination, which is beyond the scope of this treatise.

Then there are numerous sects and cults with man-made philosophies mixed with religion. Christian Science is a good example of the latter.

Dr. Hermann Sasse, in his excellent book, *Here We Stand,* has pointed out the real fundamental differences between the

Lutheran and the Reformed, particularly the Reformed Churches with strong Calvinistic leanings.

1. There is a fundamental difference in the understanding of Law and Gospel. The Fourth Article of the Augsburg Confession is about justification by faith. Luther called that the article of the standing or the falling Church. The Reformed Churches agree to a certain point. But they cannot accept that as the key to the whole Bible. For to Calvin the Gospel was after all something like a new law. And justification by faith was interpreted in the light of election.

2. Faith. To Luther faith meant trust, confidence, reliance upon, acceptance of the grace of God. To the Reformed Churches faith is essentially *obedience*. That shows the view of the Gospel as indicated above: a law to be obeyed.

3. The Church. To Luther the Church is where the Gospel is proclaimed. No very sharp distinction between visible and invisible Church. To Calvin the church is made up of the elect. That is the invisible Church. The visible Church is then made up of all who have been baptized, but who may not be elect. To Lutherans the Church is found where the Word of God is preached rightly, and where the sacraments are rightly administered, i.e., according to God's Word. The Reformed Churches have stressed church discipline and certain types of church government.

4. Lutherans stress justification by faith. The Reformed stress the sovereignty of God and predestination. "The two churches represent two different interpretations of the Gospel" (Sasse). The Reformed tend to look upon justification in the light of predestination.

5. Lutherans and Reformed differ on the doctrine of the Incarnation and therefore on the doctrine of the real presence of the Lord in the Sacrament of the Altar. The Reformed cannot see how the human personality of Jesus can hold the infinite personality of God. Lutherans believe in the union of the two natures, human and divine, after the Incarnation. The infinite did unite itself with the finite. Thus Christ can be really present in the Lord's Supper.

6. Some non-Lutheran churches deny the teaching of the total depravity of man as a result of inherited sin. It is then easy to discard infant baptism.

7. The Baptists deny the validity of infant baptism and baptism by sprinkling.

8. The Lutherans have retained something of a healthy mysticism in religion. We do not always understand; we feel deeply; we accept by faith. There is also such a thing as a healthy pietism.

9. Because of the rationalizing of the Bible, modernism has crept into the Reformed Churches, and instead of Gospel Christianity, a new paganism came into the churches. The attitude to the Bible and its central teaching about forgiveness of sin, based upon the atoning sacrifice of Jesus, and accepted in faith, determines one's outlook upon Christianity.

Read I John; II Peter; II Timothy.

Lord, keep us steadfast in Thy Word,
Curb those who fain by craft or sword
Would wrest the kingdom from Thy Son
And set at naught all He hath done.

Lord Jesus Christ, Thy power make known;
For Thou art Lord of lords alone:
Defend Thy Christendom that we
May evermore sing praise to Thee

O Comforter, of priceless worth,
Send peace and unity on earth;
Support us in our final strife.
And lead us out of death to life.

[M. LUTHER]

Some Questions and Answers

> *But sanctify the Lord God in your hearts: and be ready always to give an answer to every man that asketh you a reason of the hope that is in you with meekness and fear* (I Peter 3:15).

Questions on Chapter One:

WE BELIEVE IN GOD

1. *Why does Biblical Christianity insist so strongly upon the teaching that God is a personal God?*

Because that is the plain teaching of the Bible. Today many people make the world or the universe their God. Then there can be no call to me, no answer on my part, no faith. God is then only a figment of the mind, no objective reality. Then Christianity merely deifies the world. A personal God can address me; I can talk to Him. I can pray and be answered.

2. *Why does historic Christianity believe in a triune God?*

The answer is that Christianity and Trinitarianism go hand in hand; they arc synonymous terms. The Bible presents God as a triune God. The universal creeds of the Church present such a God. The whole idea of redemption is connected with a triune God: a God who is one in essence, in His divine substance; but who is three in persons. Unity in Trinity, used to be the saying. God is not like a triangle; but a triangle illustrates the idea of three in one. The heathen triads, like Brahma, Vishnu and Siva, are not like the Christian Trinity. Personality is lacking in the Hindu triad.

3. Can I know God?

Yes if I seek Him with my whole heart, and only then. My search will lead me to the Bible. I find God-in-Christ.

4. In the light of the teaching which we call God's providence how do we account for suffering and pain in the world? (Theodicy).

"All things work together for good to them that love God" (Romans 8:28)

Suffering is not always punishment for an individual sin. Suffering and trials have a disciplinary purpose. Suffering is part of our training. The story of Job is a good example. Also the story of Joseph shows how he was trained through his imprisonment and made fit for a great service. I Peter in the New Testament teaches that suffering puts us into fellowship with the suffering of Jesus if we are His followers. Through suffering to glory. God does not leave us alone when we suffer; He refines us.

Questions on Chapter Two·

WE BELIEVE IN THE WORKS OF GOD

A. WE BELIEVE IN REVELATION

1. Can I be sure that the Bible carries the full and complete revelation of God?

Yes, because in the Bible Christ is fully revealed.

2. What about the books "that did not get into the Bible"?

Read those that are in the Bible. As for those which are not there—like Clement's Letter to the Corinthians—they, too, can be read. But they are not divinely inspired, never claimed to be. One can feel the difference. Some of the books that were written about the same time as the Biblical books were highly regarded by the early congregations. But when it came to answer the question as to their inspiration, they could not meet the tests (see text on this matter). We have all the books in the New Testament that we need. There is a full revelation of God's will and purpose concerning our life. Nothing of importance would be added if all the apocryphal books were included.

3. *Is the Bible the Word of God or does it only contain the Word of God?*

It *is* the Word of God. That does not mean that every word in the Bible is a direct quotation of what God has said because the Bible also contains what the devil and evil men have said. But even when the devil and evil men are quoted, we learn of God's will and ways with men because we see that which is opposite to God's will. To say that the Bible *contains* the Word of God infers that here and there among the myths and folklore I find some true revelation of God. If Genesis is myth, then redemption is myth, too.

B. We Believe in God as Creator

1. *How old is the world?*

We do not know. But it is very old, according to every measurement used.

2. *How long did it take God to make the world?*

Certainly God could have made the world in six days of twenty-four hours each. Did He? Perhaps not. "In the *day* when God made heaven and earth" is a Biblical expression. And we are told that a day is like a thousand years and a thousand years like a day in the sight of God. Each day may well represent a certain period of time. That would be in keeping with the best knowledge we have as to the age of the earth.

3. *What about the theory of evolution?*

Life only begets life, as far as we know. Only a living God could bring into being such a universe as the one in which we live. It could not have made itself. Then it had a beginning. And the Bible declares: In the beginning God created!

Questions on Chapter Three

WE BELIEVE IN THE REALITY OF SIN

1. *Could not God have prevented man's fall into sin?*

Not if human beings were to be personalities such as He made them. As persons they had to have the power of choice, freedom of will. So God permitted evil in the universe He created.

2. *Is not "sin" merely a remnant of a previous jungle existence of man?*

No, for even on high cultural levels we find sin as acute as on the lower levels. Sin is revolt against God

3. *Is inherited sin really sin?*

Yes. All are sinners. The wages of sin is death. And "original sin" issues in actual sin.

4. *Is there any real difference between mortal and venial sin?*

All unforgiven sins are mortal sins. Even sins of weakness are sin. We must repent of them and seek forgiveness.

5. *What is meant by the unpardonable sin, the sin against the Holy Spirit?*

In view of the fact that the Bible teaches everywhere that God will abundantly pardon sinners who repent it is obvious that the unpardonable sin is very unusual.

Jesus referred to this sin on the occasion when He had been accused of casting out evil spirits by the power of the devil. He told His accusers then that if they were fully aware of what their accusation was really like they would have committed the unpardonable sin. See Mark 3:29; Matt. 12:31-32; Luke 12:10; I John 5:16. It is clear from these passages that the sin against the Holy Spirit, or blasphemy against the Holy Spirit, can be committed only by people who would be fully aware of the implications in calling the Spirit of God the evil spirit, and knowing what would be involved would still persist in doing it. People who still care about their soul's salvation have not committed this sin.

Questions on Chapter Four:

WE BELIEVE IN REDEMPTION

1. Do evangelical Lutherans believe that Jesus Christ is God?

Yes. The Bible declares that both directly and indirectly. The apostolic church held that belief. The creed of Nicea calls Him, "very God of very God." We pray to Jesus. We sing hymns of praise to Him as our God. We worship Him. In Him humanity and divinity meet in perfect harmony.

2. What do evangelical Lutherans believe about the atonement?

We believe that Jesus died in our stead. We call that a vicarious atonement. He made full satisfaction for us by keeping God's law and by suffering the penalty of death in our stead because we had broken the law. St. Paul declares that He took the sentence of condemnation which hung over our head and placed it over His head, and became our substitute (Col. 2:14. See, also, Is. 53).

Questions on Chapter Five:

WE BELIEVE IN THE PERSON AND WORK OF THE HOLY SPIRIT

A. WE BELIEVE IN THE HOLY SPIRIT

1. Is the Holy Spirit a person or just an influence, intuition?

The Holy Spirit is a person, the third person in the Godhead. I can pray to the Holy Spirit. He speaks to me in the Word of God.

2. What does the Holy Spirit do for me?

He makes Jesus real for me. He personalizes, individualizes the Gospel for me; He applies it to me. He helps me to understand that I am a sinner, that I need Jesus. He gives me a sensitive conscience. He stirs me up to make me realize my need of divine help. He helps me to overcome my indifference, dullness, carelessness in spiritual matters. He prompts me within to make me want to get right with God. He helps me to pray. He deepens my spiritual life. He gives me spiritual insight.

B. We Believe in a Certain Order of Salvation

1. *What do we mean by a "certain order of salvation"?*

We speak about what takes place in a person's relationship to God, himself, and other people when he is converted, becomes aware of what it is to be a Christian, and freely chooses to follow Christ.

2. *Can a person co-operate with God in his own conversion?*

He can do nothing whatsoever to earn or merit the grace of God. But he can will to resist the promptings of God's Spirit, the call of God, the influence of God's Word upon him and thus hinder his own conversion. Before conversion, man is spoken of in the Bible as being dead in trespasses and sin. He needs to be quickened by the grace of God. The first work of God's grace is to overcome man's resistance. This is accomplished by the Law and the Gospel.

3. *Can a man co-operate with God in his sanctification?*

Yes. When man has been born again by God's Spirit he is a new creature in Christ. His will is inclined to follow God's will.

4. *What, in brief, is meant by the Biblical term Justification by Faith?*

Forgiveness of sin, graciously granted by God to a sinner who repents of his sins and believes in Jesus.

5. *Can a man be regenerated by the Word of God alone?*

Yes.

6. *Should such a person be baptized?*

Of course—He that believeth and is baptized shall be saved.

7. *Can a person be regenerated in baptism?*

Yes. The Word is there, too. Where the grace of God is not resisted God can work His miracle of grace.

8. *Who must be converted?*

All who do not live in a state of grace.

9. *Can a man fall away from his regeneration, his baptismal grace, his converted state?*

Certainly. Otherwise why all the warnings in the Bible to Christians that the promises of God apply to them only if they continue in grace? Read Colossians 1:23 (especially in the translation by J. B. Phillips). See, also, II Peter 3:17-18. All the warnings to watch and pray. That he who stands must take heed lest he fall. Peter fell away from God's grace. He had to be re-instated (John 21). The teaching about eternal security easily lead to carnal security. Of course, God is able to keep us if we are willing to be kept!

10. *Do Lutheran Christians believe in the doctrine of total depravity?*

Yes, that is the plain teachings of the Bible

11. *What is meant by this doctrine?*

That man by nature is unable and even unwilling to turn to God. Man's will is out of harmony with God's will. Man can neither start nor complete his own salvation. God grants the grace to will and do. This doctrine does not deny that man is capable of civic virtues nor that he is able to do good to his neighbors. Such deeds are not meriting saving grace.

12. *Do Lutherans believe in "total and immediate sanctification"?*

No, we can find no such teaching in the Bible. On the contrary we find that the whole Christian life is a struggle between the old and the new; flesh and spirit; the natural man and the new man of God. But the Christian can reach Christian maturity in Christ, and he can gain wonderful victories as he remains in Christ (Phil. 3; II Tim.)

13. *What then would be a "normal" Christian life?*

If there is a Christian Church and Christian families the normal development from the Biblical-evangelical view would be to induct the children in such families into the Church by baptism as indicated by Matt. 28:19-20. Then to pray for them; instruct them diligently in God's Word; expect them to make their own personal choice (as, for example, the opportunity to do so in the rite of confirmation). Parents must teach their children to pray. The children should join their parents in attending church and Sunday school. They should be taught to participate in giving money for the various causes in the service of God's kingdom. They should normally be treated as members of God's household, even as we treat them as members of the families to which they belong. They should, when they are old enough, be asked to participate in the various activities of their congregation and the church at large. There is such a thing as *Christian nurture*. The baptized children of the Church should be nurtured in the Christian faith.

But suppose that in spite of all the nurture or because of lack of nurture such children stray from the Lord and His church? Then, of course, there is only one way back: the way of conversion, the return of the prodigal. *There are, no doubt, present at every church service such prodigals.* There must therefore in every sermon be a redemptive note, a call to repentance. But there must also in all proclamation of the Gospel be food for the souls who do live in communion with Christ. Not all young people are prodigals. Nor are all the others in the church prodigals. Revival and nurture must go hand in hand.

In Philippians 3:12-16, we find a powerful description of the normal Christian life.

C. We Believe in the Means of Grace

1. *What is meant by the term Means of Grace?*

That there are certain channels or vehicles through which God reaches us. They are the Word of God with its Law and Gospel, and the sacraments of Baptism and the Lord's Supper.

There are many other agencies through which God works upon us. They may be called the secondary Means of Grace; for they derive their authority from the Word of God. Such agencies are: the home, the family, the church, the ministry, our government, many and varied human experiences. There is a sense in which prayer, too, might be called a secondary Means of Grace.

Questions on Chapter Six:

WE BELIEVE IN HOLY BAPTISM

1. *What are the different points of view in the churches that admit infants to baptism?*

The Presbyterians think of infant baptism as a means of entering into covenant relationship with God. Methodists, and perhaps Congregationalists, look upon infant baptism primarily as a dedication of the child to God. Lutherans look upon infant baptism as a re-birth, the birth into God's kingdom, into Christ and the inheritance of Christ's redemption. The Roman Church believes in baptismal regeneration, but also it believes that baptism takes away, destroys original sin, and the Roman Church believes in the damnation of those who die unbaptized.

2. *Do Lutherans believe that unbaptized infants are condemned?*

We know that to enter God's kingdom a new birth is necessary (John 3), but we believe that God may have a way in which the infants who die in infancy may be regenerated and fit for heaven; for it is not your Father's will that one of these little ones should be lost (Matt. 18:14; see Matt. 18:10).

That does not excuse us if we are negligent about using the means God has prescribed for entering into discipleship.

3. *What about unbaptized heathens?*

We can only answer that God is a just God. He condemns no man unjustly. All men will be judged by the way they use the light they possess (Luke 12:47-48). That does not excuse us if we fail to participate in the command of Jesus to evangelize the whole world (Matt. 28:19-20).

Questions on Chapter Seven:

WE BELIEVE IN THE LORD'S SUPPER

1. *Why do we not admit children to the Lord's Supper?*

Because the Bible expressly declares that a person must be able to examine his own spiritual condition before he can attend the Lord's Supper (I Cor. 11:28). Children can hardly examine themselves very deeply in spiritual matters. The Lutheran Church therefore gives them a thorough instruction in the teachings of God's Word leading to confirmation (profession of faith), and then admittance to the Lord's Supper.

2. *Do Lutherans believe in the doctrine called consubstantiation in the Lord's Supper?*

No. Lutherans do not believe in consubstantiation, though we read in encyclopedias and Reformed Articles that we do. Lutherans believe in the sacramental presence of Jesus. Lutherans believe no more in consubstantiation than they do in transubstantiation.

3. *What is meant by consubstantiation?* As transubstantiation (Roman Catholic) means the changing of bread and wine to the actual flesh and blood of Jesus, so consubstantiation would mean the merging of a second element with the bread and wine so as to produce a new third element. Lutherans do not teach that doctrine. Lutherans believe in the sacramental presence of Jesus.

4. *How often should a Christian attend the Lord's Supper?*

Frequently. "As often as ye eat this bread," says the apostle Paul (I Cor. 11:26). He needs much of God's grace, much strength. The Lord's Supper is a source of assurance and strength.

5. *Why do Lutherans practice what is sometimes called closed communion?*

The "closed communion" idea is based upon the statement: Lutheran pulpits for Lutheran pastors, and Lutheran altars for Lutheran communicants. That does not mean any holier-than-thou attitude; but Lutherans are afraid of compromising the truth. Since self-examination is necessary (I Cor. 11:28), it is obvious that people must be properly instructed before they can attend communion. The Lord's Supper was instituted for disciples of Jesus. We recognize members of other churches as Christians, but their views on the Lord's Supper are usually at variance with ours and at variance among themselves.

6. *What about the preparatory service before Communion?*

Historically the preparatory service with public confession and absolution comes from the sacrament of penance as used by the Roman Church in Luther's day. It became clear that repentance, confession and absolution could not be put on a sacramental level. Scriptures know only two sacraments.

Biblically, however, there is a command that communicants *examine* themselves (I Cor. 11:28). That a repentant sinner needs to confess his sins goes without saying. But there is also provision made for *absolution* (Matt. 16:19; Matt. 18:18; John 20:23). The Christian may have forgiveness without absolution spoken by the Church (Rom. 8:16; I John 1:9). But it is of great help to a weak and struggling faith, to a burdened conscience, to be absolved through the spoken word of the pastor as he in a sense represents the Church. To the Church is given the power of the keys, the power to loose and bind. It is natural that the pastor who is called by the congregation to be the shepherd of the flock should speak the words of absolution. He *declares* the forgiveness to those who repent and confess. Unrepentant sinners do not get the benefit of the absolution. Absolution may be general or with the laying on of hands.

It is eminently fitting that there should be a preparatory service before communion. It should consist of self-examination as to one's personal relationship to Christ, repentance, confession, absolution. Then the Lord's Supper itself comes as the final pledge of God's forgiving love in Christ. The forgiven sinner should now give thanks to God for His gift, and rejoice that the burden of sin has been removed and should earnestly strive to live a God-pleasing life.

Questions on Chapter Eight:

WE BELIEVE IN CHURCH AND STATE

1. *What is the main difference between the Lutheran and the Roman Catholic conception of the Church?*

The Roman view is that the Holy Christian Church is the Roman Catholic Church. It wants to identify the Roman Church with Christianity. In Catholic theory there is only one church, the Roman Catholic. The non-Catholic "churches" are at best religious associations. That is theory. It is also Roman Catholic teaching that outside of the Roman Catholic Church there is no salvation. So said Boniface VIII in the bull *unam sanctam.*

In later statements the Roman Church seems to contradict this theory. And when recently a certain priest was disciplined for saying that those in the Roman Church who taught that salvation could be obtained outside of the Roman Church were heretics, he was disciplined largely because he had contradicted constituted authorities, higher officials in the Church. If through ignorance of the Roman Church a person remains outside of it, salvation would be possible. Wilfully and knowingly rejecting its doctrine would according to Roman teachings be fatal.

The Lutheran conception of the Church is that it is a many-branched communion. It is in reality, as we say in the Third

Article of the Apostles' Creed, the communion of saints. The following diagram might illustrate the idea.

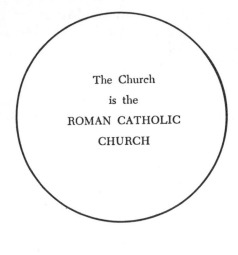

Roman Catholic conception: outside of the Church (R. C.) there is no salvation. The Roman Church from the Roman Catholic point of view is Christianity, is the kingdom of God. The Church is the hierarchy headed by the Pope. He speaks for the Church. It is not the communion of all believers on an equal footing.

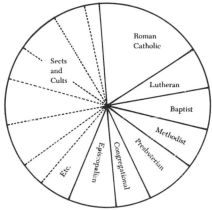

The Lutheran conception—the Church is a many-branched Communion of saints.

That does not mean that merely outward membership in the visible church organization guarantees salvation. (Diagram does not attempt to indicate actual numerical strength.)

2. What is the Lutheran attitude to government?

The Lutheran Church believes that government is needed in order to have an ordered society. It believes that government is ordained of God. But it believes that men must obey God rather than men as we read in the Book of Acts. That means when men's orders run contrary to divine orders, then Christians object. For such objections they must be willing to suffer the consequences.

Lutherans believe in the separation of church and state.

Lutherans believe that Christians may be witnesses in a trial and take an oath when required by legally constituted authorities.

Lutherans believe that Christians may participate in just wars, wars against cruel and inhuman oppression, and wars where one nation proceeds to take by force the land which we believe our Lord God gave to us.

Questions on Chapter Nine:

WE BELIEVE IN THE CHRISTIAN WAY OF LIFE

1. *Do Lutherans believe in participation in organized efforts for social betterment in the community, etc?*—Certainly. Lutherans hold education in high regard. They believe in both public and private schools. They believe in social security. But they believe in private initiative. That it is man's God-given duty and privilege to work for his own improvement as well as the improvement of others

2. *What is the Lutheran attitude towards mixed marriages?*

The Lutheran Church does not favor mixed marriages, particularly marriages between Protestants and Roman Catholics. For by the so-called *ne temere* decree of 1908 the Protestant party in a mixed marriage must promise to bring up the children of such a marriage in the Roman Catholic Church, and not try to make a Protestant of the Catholic party, and if the Catholic party dies and the Protestant remarries, and then a Protestant, the children of the first marriage are still to be Catholics.

Marriages between Protestants of different denominations are less serious if the denominations are evangelical, true to the Bible. The problem of church membership ought to be settled before the marriage takes place. It is sometimes believed that the Roman Church is the only one that gains in mixed marriages. It should be known that she loses a great number through such marriages as well as in other ways.

3. Do Lutherans believe in divine healing?

They believe in prayer, and the case of sickness can be made a subject of prayer as well as any other. But we do not neglect the use of our God-given remedies in medicines or skillful hand of surgeon or any of the other helps available.

4. What is the Lutheran attitude, in general, towards various amusements, etc?

There are certain amusements that are not necessarily sinful in themselves; but they have been monopolized by worldly people. If Christians participate in them, they might easily be led into sin. Then also there is the Christian principle of self-denial. A Christian gladly gives up questionable things to be more fully dedicated to the Lord's service. Others may easily be led astray if the Christian sets a bad example. So the Christian thinks of his weaker brother. Lutherans are not legalistic; a great deal is left to the conscience of the individual.

Question on Chapter Ten:

WE BELIEVE IN THE SECOND COMING OF OUR LORD

1. What, in general, is the Lutheran position with reference to the idea of a millennium?

The Augsburg Confession rejects any idea of an external, temporal rule of Christ. Most Lutheran theologians have been post-millennialists. There have been some pre-millennialists also. There seems to be a certain amount of freedom concerning the views held and expressed. Most Lutherans are content to rest their faith in the statement in the Second Article: "From whence He shall come to judge the quick and the dead." The Lutheran Church proclaims the good news concerning the first coming of Jesus unto salvation of souls in order that men might be ready for the second coming.

Questions on Chapter Eleven:

WE BELIEVE THAT THE LUTHERAN CHURCH IS PART OF THE HOLY CHRISTIAN CHURCH

1. *What is the Lutheran method of gaining members for the Church?*

It follows a purely Biblical method. It believes thoroughly in the method of instruction of people in the Word of God. It follows the pattern laid down both in the Old Testament and the New Testament. (See Deuteronomy, ch. 8 and ch. 11; Matt. 28:19-20.) For the purpose of helping in summarizing the teachings of the Bible it uses Luther's Catechism and other books of instruction based directly on the Bible. It follows the same method for members and non-members. It does not believe in going out to get members of other evangelical churches to join the Lutheran Church. Its doors, however, are open to all comers, and questions are gladly answered, and instruction is gladly given to all who seek it.

2. *Where was the Lutheran Church before the Reformation?*

Someone has answered: "In the Bible and in the valleys of Piedmont!"* That means, of course, that the Lutheran Church follows the Bible, and the many, who before Luther's day told the Roman Catholic Church that it had left the Bible. (In the valleys of Piedmont refers to the Waldenses who objected strenuously to the non-Biblical and extra-Biblical doctrines in the Roman Church, and who date back to Peter Waldo in France in the 12th century.—The Lutheran Church is in a straight line from the 1st Pentecost in Jerusalem.

-----

*Edman: *The Light in Dark Ages*, p. 303.

Question on Chapter Twelve:

WHEREIN EVANGELICAL LUTHERANS AGREE OR DISAGREE WITH OTHER CHRISTIANS

1. *Why does the Lutheran Church seem to be rather aloof in its relation to other churches?*

Simply because it believes that if two denominations teach almost the opposite doctrines on a certain Christian subject they cannot both be right on that particular point. If we practice exchange of pulpits, for example, the Lutheran pastor would say, in effect, to his congregation: Whatever this other pastor may say to you is certainly acceptable to me. On the sacraments, and several other points we could not accept such a view. The Lutheran Church is a conservative confessional church. It has not repudiated its confessional standards.

VARIOUS QUESTIONS

1. *Why does the Lutheran Church, rather generally, object to membership in secret societies and lodges?*

Simply because it objects to the religion of the lodge system which is, generally speaking, a religion of work-righteousness. Where Jew and Christian, Hindu and Moslem meet on the same level, without a change of heart, there can be no confession of Christ, crucified and risen, and ever reigning Lord.

2. *Does not the Lutheran Church then believe in the equality of all men before God?*

Certainly. But it believes in the sinfulness of all men, Jews and Gentiles, in the need of repentance for all men, and it believes that Jesus Christ is the only Savior of the world. If that makes the Lutheran Church intolerant, then the Bible is intolerant, too; for it teaches only one way of salvation.

3. *But do the lodges have a religion?*

From their own rituals and writings it is evident that they have a religion. To their humanitarian programs there can be no objection. Christians are warned not to be unequally yoked together with unbelievers (II Cor. 6:14).

SUGGESTED BIBLE READINGS FOR THOSE WHO PREPARE FOR CHURCH MEMBERSHIP

The Gospel According to St. Mark	I and II Timothy
Philippians	Titus
Galatians	I John

Throughout the text there are numerous Bible references, and certain Bible readings are suggested at the end of each chapter. Use the references!

PART THREE

Dr. Martin Luther's Small Catechism

PART I

The Ten Commandments

THE INTRODUCTION

I am the Lord thy God.

THE FIRST COMMANDMENT

Thou shalt have no other gods before me.

What does this mean?

We should fear, love, and trust in God above all things.

THE SECOND COMMANDMENT

Thou shalt not take the name of the Lord thy God in vain; for the Lord will not hold him guiltless that taketh His name in vain.

What does this mean?

We should fear and love God so that we do not curse, swear, conjure, lie, or deceive, by His name, but call upon Him in every time of need, and worship Him with prayer, praise, and thanksgiving

THE THIRD COMMANDMENT

Remember the Sabbath day, to keep it holy.

What does this mean?

We should fear and love God so that we do not despise His Word and the preaching of the same, but deem it holy, and gladly hear and learn it.

THE FOURTH COMMANDMENT

Honor thy father and thy mother, that thy days may be long upon the land which the Lord thy God giveth thee.

What does this mean?

We should fear and love God so that we do not despise our parents and superiors, nor provoke them to anger, but honor, serve, obey, love, and esteem them.

THE FIFTH COMMANDMENT

Thou shalt not kill.

What does this mean?

We should fear and love God so that we do our neighbor no bodily harm nor cause him any suffering, but help and befriend him in every need.

THE SIXTH COMMANDMENT

Thou shalt not commit adultery.

What does this mean?

We should fear and love God so that we lead a chaste and pure life in word and deed, and that husband and wife love and honor each other.

THE SEVENTH COMMANDMENT

Thou shalt not steal.

What does this mean?

We should fear and love God so that we do not rob our neighbor of his money or property, nor bring them into our possession by unfair dealing or fraud, but help him to improve and protect his property and living.

THE EIGHTH COMMANDMENT

Thou shalt not bear false witness against thy neighbor.

What does this mean?

We should fear and love God so that we do not deceitfully belie, betray, backbite, nor slander our neighbor, but apologize for him, speak well of him, and put the most charitable construction on all that he does.

THE NINTH COMMANDMENT

Thou shalt not covet thy neighbor's house.

What does this mean?

We should fear and love God so that we do not seek by craftiness to gain possession of our neighbor's inheritance or home nor obtain them under pretense of a legal right, but assist and serve him in keeping the same.

THE TENTH COMMANDMENT

Thou shalt not covet thy neighbor's wife, nor his manservant, nor his maidservant, nor his cattle, nor anything that is thy neighbor's.

What does this mean?

We should fear and love God so that we do not estrange or entice away our neighbor's wife, servants, or cattle, but seek to have them remain and discharge their duty to him.

THE CONCLUSION

What does God declare concerning all these Commandments?

He says: I the Lord thy God am a jealous God, visiting the iniquity of the fathers upon the children unto the third and fourth generation of them that hate me; and showing mercy unto thousands of them that love me and keep my commandments.

What does this mean?

God threatens to punish all who transgress these commandments. We should, therefore, fear His wrath, and in no wise disobey them. But He promises grace and every blessing to all who keep them. We should, therefore, love Him, trust in Him, and gladly keep His commandments.

PART II

The Creed

THE FIRST ARTICLE

OF CREATION

I believe in God the Father almighty, maker of heaven and earth.

What does this mean?

I believe that God has created me and all that exists; that He has given and still preserves to me my body and soul, my eyes and ears, and all my members, my reason and all the powers of my soul, together with food and raiment, home and family, and all my property; that He daily provides abundantly for all the needs of my life, protects me from all danger, and guards and keeps me from all evil; and that He does this purely out of fatherly and divine goodness and mercy, without any merit or worthiness in me; for all of which I am in duty bound to thank, praise, serve, and obey Him. This is most certainly true.

THE SECOND ARTICLE

OF REDEMPTION

And in Jesus Christ His only Son, our Lord; who was conceived by the Holy Spirit, born of the Virgin Mary; suffered under Pontius Pilate, was crucified, dead, and buried; He descended into hell; the third day He rose again from the dead; He ascended into heaven, and sitteth on the right hand of God the Father almighty; from thence He shall come to judge the quick and the dead.

What does this mean?

I believe that Jesus Christ, true God, begotten of the Father from eternity, and also true Man, born of the Virgin Mary,

is my Lord; who has redeemed me, a lost and condemned creature, bought me and freed me from all sins, from death, and
from the power of the devil; not with silver and gold, but with
His holy and precious blood, and with His innocent sufferings
and death; in order that I might be His own, live under Him
in His kingdom, and serve Him in everlasting righteousness,
innocence, and blessedness; even as He is risen from the dead,
and lives and reigns to all eternity. This is most certainly true.

THE THIRD ARTICLE

OF SANCTIFICATION

I believe in the Holy Spirit; the holy Christian Church, the
Communion of Saints; the forgiveness of sins; the resurrection
of the body; and the life everlasting.

What does this mean?

I believe that I cannot by my own reason or strength believe in Jesus Christ my Lord, or come to Him; but the Holy
Spirit has called me through the Gospel, enlightened me with
His gifts, and sanctified and preserved me in the true faith;
in like manner as He calls, gathers, enlightens, and sanctifies
the whole Christian Church on earth, and preserves it in
union with Jesus Christ in the one true faith; in which Christian Church He daily forgives abundantly all my sins, and
the sins of all believers, and at the last day will rise up me
and all the dead, and will grant everlasting life to me and to
all who believe in Christ. This is most certainly true.

PART III

The Lord's Prayer

THE INTRODUCTION

Our Father, who art in heaven.

What does this mean?

God thereby tenderly encourages us to believe that He is truly our Father, and that we are truly His children, so that we may boldly and confidently come to Him in prayer, even as beloved children come to their dear father.

THE FIRST PETITION

Hallowed be Thy name.

What does this mean?

God's name is indeed holy in itself; but we pray in this petition that it may be hallowed also among us.

How is this done?

When the Word of God is taught in its truth and purity and we, as God's children, lead holy lives, in accordance with it. This grant us, dear Father in heaven! But whoever teaches and lives otherwise than God's Word teaches, profanes the name of God among us. From this preserve us, heavenly Father!

THE SECOND PETITION

Thy kingdom come.

What does this mean?

The kingdom of God comes indeed of itself, without our prayer; but we pray in this petition that it may come also to us.

How is this done?

When our heavenly Father gives us His Holy Spirit, so that by His grace we believe His holy Word, and live a godly life here on earth, and in heaven for ever.

THE THIRD PETITION

Thy will be done on earth, as it is in heaven.

What does this mean?

The good and gracious will of God is done indeed without our prayer; but we pray in this petition that it may be done also among us.

How is this done?

When God destroys and brings to naught every evil counsel and purpose of the devil, the world, and our own flesh, which would hinder us from hallowing His name, and prevent the coming of His kingdom; and when He strengthens us and keeps us steadfast in His Word and in faith, even unto our end. This is His good and gracious will.

THE FOURTH PETITION

Give us this day our daily bread.

What does this mean?

God indeed gives daily bread to all men, even to the wicked, without our prayer; but we pray in this petition that He would lead us to acknowledge our daily bread as His gift, and to receive it with thanksgiving.

What is meant by daily bread?

Everything that is required to satisfy our bodily needs; such as food and raiment, house and home, fields and flocks, money and goods; pious parents, children, and servants; godly and faithful rulers, good government; seasonable weather, peace and health; order and honor; true friends, good neighbors, and the like.

THE FIFTH PETITION

And forgive us our trespasses, as we forgive those who trespass against us.

What does this mean?

We pray in this petition that our heavenly Father would

not regard our sins nor because of them deny our prayers; for we neither merit nor are worthy of those things for which we pray; but that He would grant us all things through grace, even though we sin daily, and deserve nothing but punishment. And certainly we, on our part, will heartily forgive, and gladly do good to those who may sin against us.

THE SIXTH PETITION

And lead us not into temptation.

What does this mean?

God indeed tempts no one to sin; but we pray in this petition that God would so guard and preserve us, that the devil, the world, and our own flesh may not deceive us, nor lead us into error and unbelief, despair, and other great and shameful sins; but that, when so tempted, we may finally prevail and gain the victory.

THE SEVENTH PETITION

But deliver us from evil.

What does this mean?

We pray in this petition, as in a summary, that our heavenly Father would deliver us from all manner of evil, whether it affect body or soul, property or reputation, and at last, when the hour of death shall come, grant us a blessed end, and graciously take us from this world of sorrow to Himself in heaven.

THE CONCLUSION

For Thine is the kingdom, and the power, and the glory, for ever and ever. Amen.

What does the word "Amen" mean?

It means that I should be assured that such petitions are acceptable to our heavenly Father, and are heard by Him; for He Himself has commanded us to pray in this manner, and has promised to hear us. Amen, Amen, that is, Yea, yea, it shall be so.

PART IV

The Sacrament of Baptism

I

WHAT IS BAPTISM?

Baptism is not simply water, but it is the water used according to God's command and connected with God's word.

What is this word of God?

It is the word of our Lord Jesus Christ, as recorded in the last chapter of Matthew: "Go ye therefore, and make disciples of all the nations, baptizing them into the name of the Father and of the Son and of the Holy Spirit."

II

WHAT GIFTS OR BENEFITS DOES BAPTISM BESTOW?

It works forgiveness of sins, delivers from death and the devil, and gives everlasting salvation to all who believe, as the word and promise of God declare.

What is this word and promise of God?

It is the word of our Lord Jesus Christ, as recorded in the last chapter of Mark: "He that believeth and is baptized shall be saved; but he that disbelieveth shall be condemned."

III

HOW CAN WATER DO SUCH GREAT THINGS?

It is not the water, indeed, that does such great things, but the word of God, connected with the water, and our faith which relies on that word of God. For without the word of God, it is simply water and no baptism. But when connected with the word of God, it is a baptism, that is, a gracious water of life and a washing of regeneration in the Holy Spirit, as

St. Paul says to Titus, in the third chapter: "According to His mercy He saved us, through the washing of regeneration and renewing of the Holy Spirit, which He poured out upon us richly, through Jesus Christ our Savior; that, being justified by His grace, we might be made heirs according to the hope of eternal life. This is a faithful saying."

IV

WHAT DOES SUCH BAPTIZING WITH WATER SIGNIFY?

It signifies that the old Adam in us, together with all sins and evil lusts, should be drowned by daily sorrow and repentance, and be put to death; and that the new man should daily come forth and rise, to live before God in righteousness and holiness for ever.

Where is it so written?

St. Paul, in the sixth chapter of the Epistle to the Romans, says: "We were buried therefore with him through baptism into death: that like as Christ was raised from the dead through the glory of the Father, so we also might walk in newness of life."

OF CONFESSION

What is Confession?

Confession consists of two parts: the one is that we confess our sins; the other, that we receive absolution or forgiveness from the pastor as from God Himself, in no wise doubting but firmly believing, that our sins are thereby forgiven before God in heaven.

What sins should we confess?

Before God we should acknowledge ourselves guilty of all manner of sins, even of those of which we are not aware, as we do in the Lord's Prayer. To the pastor we should confess only those sins which we know and feel in our hearts.

What are such sins?

Here examine yourself in the light of the Ten Commandments, whether as father or mother, son or daughter, master or servant, you have been disobedient, unfaithful, slothful, ill-tempered, unchaste, or quarrelsome, or whether you have injured anyone by word or deed, stolen, neglected, or wasted aught, or done any other evil.

PART V

The Sacrament of the Altar

I

WHAT IS THE SACRAMENT OF THE ALTAR?

It is the true Body and Blood of our Lord Jesus Christ, under the bread and wine, given unto us Christians to eat and to drink, as it was instituted by Christ Himself.

Where is it so written?

The holy Evangelists, Matthew, Mark, and Luke, together with St. Paul, write thus:

"Our Lord Jesus Christ, in the night in which He was betrayed, took bread; and when He had given thanks, He brake it and gave it to His disciples, saying, Take, eat; this is my body, which is given for you; this do in remembrance of me.

"After the same manner, also, He took the cup, when He had supped, and when He had given thanks, He gave it to them, saying, Drink ye all of it; this cup is the New Testament in my Blood, which is shed for you, and for many, for the remission of sins; this do, as oft as ye drink it, in remembrance of me."

II

WHAT IS THE BENEFIT OF SUCH EATING AND DRINKING?

It is pointed out in these words: "Given and shed for you for the remission of sins." Through these words the remission of sins, life and salvation are given unto us in the Sacrament; for where there is remission of sins, there is also life and salvation.

III

HOW CAN THE BODILY EATING AND DRINKING PRODUCE SUCH GREAT BENEFITS?

The eating and drinking, indeed, do not produce them, but the words: "Given and shed for you for the remission of sins." For besides the bodily eating and drinking, these words are the chief thing in the Sacrament; and he who believes them has what they say and declare, namely, the remission of sins.

IV

WHO, THEN, RECEIVES THE SACRAMENT WORTHILY?

Fasting and bodily preparation are indeed a good outward discipline, but he is truly worthy and well prepared who believes these words: "Given and shed for you for the remission of sins." But he who does not believe these words or who doubts them is unworthy and unprepared; for the words: "For you," require truly believing hearts.